LEFT-HEARTED, RIGHT-MINDED

WHY CONSERVATIVE POLICIES ARE THE BEST WAY TO ACHIEVE LIBERAL IDEALS

DAVID B. COHEN

Southeast Press

ISBN-10: 0615635636
ISBN-13: 978-0615635637 (Southeast Press)

CONTENTS

ABOUT THE AUTHOR

David B. Cohen is an attorney and a contributor to *The Daily Caller*. He served in the Bush Administration as the U.S. Representative to the Pacific Community, as Deputy Assistant Secretary of the Interior and as a member of President Bush's Advisory Commission on Asian Americans and Pacific Islanders.

Prior to joining the Bush Administration, Cohen was a partner in the law firm of Sidley Austin. Cohen simultaneously earned an M.B.A. from the Wharton School and a Juris Doctor degree from the University of Pennsylvania Law School. He previously earned three other degrees, including a Master's degree, from the University of Pennsylvania—all by the age of 21. Cohen is the co-author of *Modern Business Law* and *Business and its Legal Environment*. He holds the chiefly title of *Papali'i* in the Samoan culture.

1 LIBERAL DAVE

Allow me to introduce you to Liberal Dave. Liberal Dave is near and dear to my heart. Actually, Liberal Dave is me—or, more accurately, the person I used to be. In many ways, though, I am still Liberal Dave. Although I no longer identify myself as a liberal, I still care about most of the same things I cared about when I was Liberal Dave. I even hold a number of the same policy positions that Liberal Dave holds. Believe it or not, Liberal Dave is in some ways more conservative than ConservaDave, a really cool guy to whom I will introduce you a little later. For example, Liberal Dave was in favor of the death penalty and ConservaDave is not. More on that later, but go figure. Also, ConservaDave is a vegetarian—out of compassion for animals, no less, rather than for his own health.

I am still very fond of Liberal Dave and, even though my views today largely differ from Liberal Dave's views, I still have a great deal of respect for him. The theme of this book is not "I used to be a liberal idiot until I wised up and became a conservative." This book is more about how Liberal Dave and ConservaDave can find common ground and can coexist—even in the same body.

Liberal Dave was born and raised a Democrat. He had humble origins. (He perhaps became somewhat conceited later in life, but originally he was humble.) He believed that he had a normal childhood, although it may not appear normal on paper. Liberal Dave was born out of wedlock to a Jewish mother and a Samoan father. Liberal Dave's mother raised him in inner city Washington, D.C. after his father left. (Liberal Dave's father would later come back into his life, and would eventually even bring him back to his village in Samoa to be bestowed a chiefly title; but that story is best saved for when Liberal Dave gets around to writing his autobiography.) The burden of single motherhood left Liberal Dave's mother no choice but to continue living at home with her parents and younger brother. By leaving, Liberal Dave's Samoan father therefore virtually guaranteed that Liberal Dave would be raised by an extended family—Samoan style, one could say, except that the extended family in this case was Jewish.

When Liberal Dave was growing up, everyone in his house (apartment, actually) was a Democrat. Liberal Dave's extended family included three hardcore union members: his grandfather, a printer, was a lifelong member of the old International Typographical Union; his uncle Bill, a mailer for *The Washington Post*, was a Teamster; and his mother, a fourth grade teacher at Anne Beers Elementary School in Southeast D.C., was a member of the American Federation of Teachers. Those familiar with teachers union politics will know that the AFT was historically more radical than the larger National Education Association.

Liberal Dave's grandfather wouldn't even get his hair cut at a non-union barber shop. One of the seminal events that Liberal Dave remembers from growing up was the violent *Washington Post* strike, in which the pressmen sabotaged the presses before walking out. Liberal Dave's grandfather and Uncle Bill were both working at the *Post* at the time. The Teamsters, Uncle Bill's union, went on strike and the ITU, his grandfather's union, was locked out. *Washingtonian* magazine did story on the strike, featuring a large photo of Uncle Bill walking his little pet schnauzer on the picket line. It was a great picture, and Liberal Dave was very proud of his uncle.

That strike was a collision between two great liberal institutions that helped shape Liberal Dave's political consciousness: trade unionism and *The Washington Post*. Although Liberal Dave was only a kid during Watergate, he avidly followed what was going on. He idolized the *Post*'s Bob Woodward, Carl Bernstein, and Ben Bradlee. Their heroic exploits in bringing down the evil Republican President Richard Nixon inspired Liberal Dave to want to become a journalist (and, of course, join the Newspaper Guild, the union for reporters). Liberal Dave loved *The Washington Post*, his hometown newspaper. He read it regularly since elementary school, at first mostly to follow his beloved Washington Redskins. (An often frustrating love of the Washington Redskins, by the way, is one of the main areas of common ground between Liberal Dave and ConservaDave.) By the time of the great *Post* strike, young Liberal Dave looked forward each morning to reading not only the paper's sports section, but its international news, its local news, the Style section, Doonesbury—almost everything but the business section. Liberal Dave had no interest in business. The acclaim that the *Post* received as a result of the Watergate scandal made Liberal Dave even more proud of his local newspaper, and helped alleviate his underlying Washingtonian inferiority complex regarding New York, *The New York Times*, and all things Big Apple.

Liberal Dave was, to say the least, conflicted by the *Post* strike. Had *The Washington Post* been a person, it would have been *persona non grata* in Liberal Dave's home during the strike. Liberal Dave's grandfather and Uncle Bill were at war with the *Post*, and everyone else in the family was expected, out of loyalty, to be at war with the *Post* as well. That was all well and good, but the *Post* had become Liberal Dave's great inspiration and cherished morning ritual. In the days before 24-hour cable news, Liberal Dave didn't think that he could live without his daily *Washington Post* fix. And so he continued to read the *Post*, surreptitiously, on the side. But, as Liberal Dave would want you to know, as a good liberal he felt *very guilty* about it. Needless to say, he felt very relieved when the strike finally ended.

Not only was Liberal Dave's childhood household exclusively Democratic, but the entire neighborhood for miles on end was almost exclusively Democratic. Southeast Washington was, at the time, rapidly changing from a largely African-American but integrated working class neighborhood to an almost exclusively African-American poor neighborhood. When it came time for him to start school, Liberal Dave was sent to a Jewish parochial school in Northwest Washington rather than the virtually all-black Stanton Elementary School in his Southeast Washington neighborhood. Liberal Dave's family was not religious. They sent him to religious school in order to get the type of quality education that he was not likely to receive in D.C.'s notorious public school system. They were also concerned that Liberal Dave would be ostracized as the only Jewish-Samoan kid, and one of a handful of non-black kids, at Stanton. Given historical Jewish voting patterns, Liberal Dave probably would have encountered as many kids whose parents voted Republican at Stanton as he did at his Jewish school.

Even after the family moved outside of the city to Maryland, there weren't many Republicans around. Career civil servants for the federal government have traditionally made up, by far, the largest segment of the workforce for the Washington, D.C. metropolitan area. This group has historically had a strong tendency to vote Democratic. Although federal workers are generally thought of as white collar employees, the Feds employ a large number of blue collar workers as well. Before Liberal Dave was born, his grandfather had moved the family from New York to Washington after he got a job as a printer at the Government Printing Office. He spent almost his entire career working the graveyard shift at the

GPO, working while the rest of the family slept, sleeping while the rest of family was going about its day.

While Liberal Dave's family was proudly union and definitely identified with the Democrats, it was not a highly politicized household. Like most working families, Liberal Dave's family had better things to worry about. There were no great political debates around the dinner table—a lot of yelling, sure, but not about anything important. Liberal Dave's grandmother was fond of saying, "The rich are the same as the rest of us. They put their pants on one leg at a time." Actually, that was her clean version. She also had another version having to do with something smelling just as bad as something else, but that need not be quoted verbatim here. But Liberal Dave's grandmother was no fire-breathing class warrior. If she or anyone else in the family ever voted, Liberal Dave wasn't aware of it. Still, virtually every political signal Liberal Dave received growing up, from family to neighborhood to school to media, tended to support his left-of-center view of the world. As an idealistic, *Post*-reading adolescent coming of age in the heady post-Watergate era, Liberal Dave began to develop more of a political consciousness than any of his elders at home.

Growing up in Washington during that period made it easy to develop a political consciousness. The riots following the assassination of Dr. Martin Luther King; violent anti-war demonstrations; the Watergate hearings: for Washingtonians, this was all local news. Liberal Dave was just a kid when these things were going on. But to the extent that he understood them, they captured his imagination; he wished that he had been older, so he could have participated in the excitement. When Liberal Dave was a high school student in nearby Maryland in the late 1970s, the protest music of the 1960s was still in heavy rotation on the radio. It was hard not to be inspired by the music that served as the soundtrack for the momentous events of the era: *Tin soldiers and Nix-on com-ing. We're finally on our own. This summer I hear the drum-ming. Four dead in O-hi-o.*[1] Protest music had become popular music, stirring the hearts of young people. *We can change the world!*[2]

It was an exciting time to be coming into one's political awareness, especially for someone with young Liberal Dave's view of the world. Nixon resigns. Good riddance! The Vietnam War ends. How could that possibly be bad? The post-Watergate Congressional elections sweep Democratic reformers into office on a wave of hope and change, with a large class of promising freshmen like Christopher Dodd and Jack Murtha vowing to clean up the mess of Republican corruption. *The times they are a-changin'!*[3]

Music wasn't the only aspect of popular culture that helped to solidify Liberal Dave's developing political views. His favorite TV show—indeed, America's favorite TV show—was "All in the Family." Sure, Archie Bunker was a bigot, but we were laughing *at* him, not with him. And we all knew that Norman Lear and Bud Yorkin, the show's producers, had their hearts in the right place— they were *liberals*. In fact, this was the era when the American public first became widely aware that most of the people behind the popular culture that we enjoyed so much—especially the culture that appealed to the young—were liberals. The people who sang the songs we sang along to, who directed and starred in the movies we loved, who produced and acted in the TV shows we watched each week, who wrote the books that we read (for those who bothered to read books), seemed to be overwhelmingly liberal. These were the coolest people in our society, the people whose lead we wanted to follow, the people whom we wanted to be like.

"All in the Family" was eventually replaced as Liberal Dave's favorite TV show by "Saturday Night Live." Liberal Dave used to love Chevy Chase's portrayal of Republican President Ford as a bewildered, clumsy, bumbling idiot. But lest you think they joked only about Republicans, they joked about Democrat Jimmy Carter as well—about how he was such an incredibly cool and intelligent guy. Dan Aykroyd's Jimmy Carter could quote Bob Dylan and could offer incredibly detailed instructions to help a drug-addled caller down from a "bad trip." Among the youthful demographic of "Saturday Night Live," there is no doubt who would have won an election between Chevy Chase's Gerald Ford and Dan Aykroyd's Jimmy Carter. Liberal Dave, still too young to vote, was pleased that the real election turned out the same way.

By the time he got to college, Liberal Dave was still, well, Liberal Dave. He was fortunate enough to earn a full-tuition scholarship to an expensive Ivy League school, the University of Pennsylvania. Penn, as it is known, was founded in Philadelphia by Benjamin Franklin and claims to be the first university in the U.S. All of those years of reading *The Washington Post* had undoubtedly helped to develop Liberal Dave's reading and cognitive skills to the point where he could be accepted into such a fine university. Penn was *not* to be confused, as most Penn students would snobbishly admonish you, with Penn State. *They're* the ones with the good football team, we would sniff condescendingly.

As a freshman, Liberal Dave followed his ambition and joined *The Daily Pennsylvanian*, Penn's award-winning daily newspaper. Corny T-shirts about how different professions "do it" were in vogue back then ("accountants do it with double entry"); Liberal Dave used to proudly wear a T-shirt around campus proclaiming: *"The Daily Pennsylvanian*: We Do It Every Day." If only. In any event, Liberal Dave was certainly proud and excited to be a part of the *DP*.

One of Liberal Dave's early assignments was to cover the budding protest movement to get the university endowment to sell off its stock in companies that did business with South Africa. (At the time, of course, Nelson Mandela was still languishing in prison and blacks continued to suffer segregation and oppression under apartheid.) While paying lip service to journalistic objectivity, Liberal Dave got swept up in the excitement and romance of the good guys (campus protest leaders) building a movement to take on the bad guys (old, white university trustees who claimed that they had a fiduciary duty to prevent the university endowment from losing money). Liberal Dave eventually became City Editor of the DP, where he got to cover the political battles between Philadelphia's "reformers," as so designated by *The Philadelphia Inquirer* (good), and the political machine of Mayor Frank Rizzo (bad).

Liberal Dave tried his hand at writing columns for the DP. He caused quite a stir when he wrote a column on losing his religion on Yom Kippur, the Day of Atonement on which religious Jews do not eat or drink. Liberal Dave wrote about how he abandoned his fast in the middle of Yom Kippur "with the bite of an apple" because he realized that he no longer believed in Judaism. The column triggered a barrage of angry letters from Penn's large Jewish community, including from the rabbi at Penn's Jewish center. Liberal Dave's secret, though, was that the column was actually fictional. He had fasted for all of Yom Kippur that year, just as he had every year and would continue to do every year (and as ConservaDave would do every year).

Liberal Dave was a little fuzzy in his own mind, even at the time, about what exactly motivated him to write the column. He did think that the rootlessness that one would undoubtedly feel upon abandoning one's religion would make for an interesting column, especially if recounted in the first person by one who had actually done it. Also, at some level, he probably felt that it was fashionable to portray himself as having abandoned his religion—it would make him appear to be more intellectual, more radical. Didn't John Lennon, in his wildly popular utopian anthem "Imagine," yearn for a world with no religion? Who didn't admire John Lennon? Liberal Dave, of course, didn't have the courage to actually do what he said he did in his column. He was posing, hedging his bets by fasting, and hoping (make that praying) that his fasting would offset any damage that his column might have done to his standing upstairs.

When President Reagan was shot, one of Liberal Dave's best friends, a fellow DP reporter, reacted as follows in an op-ed piece: "I hope he dies." At the time, Liberal Dave did not see anything wrong with that. Liberal Dave did not wish death on President Reagan (although, as he would hasten to add just to make sure that you knew, he was no fan of Reagan). For whatever reason, Liberal Dave did not find his friend's quote to be as jarring as (the yet-to-be-born) ConservaDave would have found it. (Thoughts on that later.) In Liberal Dave's mind, his friend had an absolute right to express his opinion and the DP's eventual apology for publishing the column was an unfortunate capitulation to Reagan-loving fascists who would curb free expression. The "I hope he dies" quote was included in a national news magazine's compilation of quotes reacting to the Reagan shooting. Liberal Dave and his friend used to laugh about how the friend's quote was juxtaposed against a much more restrained quote—from Iran's Ayatollah Khomeini.

At Penn, Liberal Dave's horizons were broadened as he had the opportunity to meet, for the first time, a stunningly diverse group of people. There were rich liberals, whose parents actually could afford Penn's outrageous tuition bill. There were liberals who, like Liberal Dave, were there thanks to Penn's generous financial aid program. There were liberals from the inner city, liberals from the suburbs, and liberals from the country. There were liberal exchange students from all around the world. There were liberal professors and liberal administrators. In short, the spectacular diversity of America was on full display on that one college campus.

Now, of course I'm being a little flippant about how Penn was such a diverse community in which almost everyone conformed to the same political belief system. One is likely to meet mostly liberals at most college campuses for a variety of reasons. For one thing, college students are at an age where they're more likely to be liberal. Most students enter a college like Penn without yet having had significant financial responsibilities, making it easier for them to be seduced by the advertised benefits of major socials programs than to appreciate the costs. They arrive on campus fresh from having their education delivered by high school teachers, who then pass the baton seamlessly to college professors. Not to suggest that high school teachers and college professors tend to lean liberal, but….well, perhaps I do mean to suggest that.[4] Also, adolescents and young adults are naturally rebellious, and media and popular culture tend to suggest to the young that liberals represent the rebellion and conservatives the ones who must be rebelled against. Even during those periods when the Democrats control the presidency and both houses of Congress, the popular culture still manages to send the message that supporting the Democrats is tantamount to rebelling against the status quo.

Referring to the overwhelming majority of people in Liberal Dave's college community as "liberals" is not to suggest that they were all vocally political. The majority of students, like the majority of people everywhere, were not overly preoccupied with politics. They had more important things to worry about, like getting into Med School and getting laid. But had you pressed them for their political views, Liberal Dave was convinced that most would have revealed themselves to have been decidedly liberal. And like Liberal Dave's childhood home in Southeast D.C., Penn's West Philadelphia campus was surrounded for miles around by communities that voted overwhelmingly Democratic.

Although Liberal Dave assumed that most of his professors were liberal, it did not appear to him that they were trying to indoctrinate him. (Perhaps ConservaDave would have had a stronger nose for that type of thing.) There was one class in which the professor drew a graph demonstrating that as wages went up, the number of workers that employers would be willing to hire went down. "So," said the professor, "When the Republicans say that raising the minimum wage increases unemployment, they're actually correct." The professor did not, however, appear to be saying this out of admiration for Republicans. It was more in the nature of a "fun fact," as if to say: "Contrary to what we all would have expected, the Republicans have made a point that is actually correct." Or as if to say: "The Republicans have gotten something correct, just as idiot savants get some things correct, or just as broken clocks are correct twice a day." It was in the spirit of television talk show host John McLaughlin sarcastically congratulating one of his guest pundits for "blundering into the truth." Well, at least that's the way that Liberal Dave interpreted his professor's remark.

Now, it is possible that Liberal Dave simply assumed that the overwhelming majority of his classmates and professors were liberal because the overwhelming majority of people that he had encountered in his life to that point were liberal. When people grow up in an environment where everyone thinks in the same way, there is perhaps a natural tendency to assume that everyone else thinks that way as well. There was little in the popular culture or media that Liberal Dave had been exposed to that would have suggested otherwise. This might explain the genuine bewilderment that Liberal Dave experienced on those occasions at Penn when he met people who revealed themselves—gird your loins—*not* to be liberal.

Sure, Liberal Dave knew that there were Republicans "out there." He had read about them. He knew that some had been elected to office—after all, there had to be someone to represent all of the rich, greedy, heartless, stupid, mean-spirited racists that he had heard about. But they existed for him more in theory than in the flesh. Before college, he had never actually had a political discussion with someone who identified himself as a Republican or a conservative.

When Liberal Dave finally did have meaningful contact with Republicans, he was surprised by where he found them. At *The Daily Pennsylvanian*, which Liberal Dave had assumed to be a sanctuary of like-minded Woodward & Bernstein wannabes who

11

wanted to change the world (i.e. make it more liberal), Liberal Dave was surprised to learn that one of his friends and fellow reporters was a Republican. This person—we'll give him the assumed name of "Scott" to shield him from damage to his reputation and questions about his character—was actually a really nice guy. Scott was very clean cut and a little square, so in retrospect, maybe it all made sense. Scott's startling revelation of his Republicanism did not cause Liberal Dave to like him any less, but Liberal Dave could never figure out why Scott would want to be a Republican. Who would want to be so uncool? Liberal Dave's other friend at the DP—the one who would later become famous for wishing death on President Reagan—would delight in pointing out to Scott that Republicans are "Neanderthals." Scott would laugh along and take it in good cheer, even though Mr. "Death to Reagan" actually meant it.

Liberal Dave was even more surprised when, in the Pennsylvania gubernatorial race, *The Daily Pennsylvanian* ended up endorsing Republican Dick Thornburgh. Liberal Dave could not understand this decision, which was made by the upperclassmen on the DP's editorial board. Was there not a Democrat in the race? Of course, there *was* a Democrat in the race: Pete Flaherty, the perfectly respectable mayor of Pittsburgh. Why, then, would the DP refuse to endorse the Democrat? Thornburgh was a former U.S. Attorney who promised to crack down on corruption in Pennsylvania. Whatever. Could corruption in Pennsylvania really have been such a big issue to justify endorsing a freaking Republican? Still, Liberal Dave knew all of the editorial board members that voted to endorse Thornburgh (who, no doubt on the strength of the DP endorsement, went on to win the race); he knew them to be decent people, and his respect for them was somehow not diminished by their puzzling support for a Neanderthal.

From time to time thereafter, Liberal Dave would occasionally learn that people whom he liked and respected were in fact

Republicans. In each case, that revelation did not make Liberal Dave like or respect these people less. I suppose that one's personal experience with people tends to trump one's preconceived notions, especially when one gets to know the people first and their politics later.

Liberal Dave learned that the GOP had infiltrated not only his circle of friends, but his family as well. Two of Liberal Dave's uncles on his Samoan side—his father's brothers—were living in Philadelphia. One of these uncles, Uncle Titi, was apolitical. He drove a taxicab, and riding along in the front passenger seat became a fun (and sometimes hair-raising) way for Liberal Dave to tour the city. But Liberal Dave's other uncle, Uncle Vainu'upo, had run for Mayor of Philadelphia years before—as a *Republican*. He campaigned as the "Samoan Prince," wearing a Western suit and tie with a floral Samoan *lava lava* wrapped around his waist. This had happened when Liberal Dave was a kid, and his mother was not in touch with his Samoan relatives in Philadelphia at the time. Liberal Dave had had no idea that his own uncle was a Republican running for Mayor of Philadelphia. Liberal Dave never discussed politics with Uncle Vainu'upo. He wondered to himself why his uncle would be a Republican, but just figured (in the condescending manner of a young Ivy League student who knew everything) that the old man didn't know any better.

One day Uncle Vainu'upo took his sons Faleolo, Talavou and Titi—Liberal Dave's cousins—to a town hall meeting with Republican Senator John Heinz in West Philadelphia. Liberal Dave tagged along. The crowd was almost all African American, reflecting the make-up of the neighborhood. Uncle Vainu'upo's party, including Liberal Dave, stood out, wearing brightly colored Polynesian shirts designed for a different climate. Senator Heinz, working his way through the crowd and shaking hands before taking the stage, came across the Samoan contingent and asked: "What organization do you represent?"

A little puzzled, Uncle Vainu'upo responded: "We're just Republicans."

That was too much for Liberal Dave, who at the time would have sooner died than have anyone think that he was a Republican. Liberal Dave cut in defensively: "I'm not. I'm a Democrat." Uncle Vainu'upo looked embarrassed, and Liberal Dave immediately felt bad. As a Samoan chief, Uncle Vainu'upo wasn't used to being contradicted by younger members of his own family—especially in front of distinguished visitors. Liberal Dave realized that he had needlessly disrespected his uncle, and as much as he hated the thought of being lumped in with Republicans, he thought: "Would it have killed me to have just kept my mouth shut?"

So, Liberal Dave learned that while he didn't understand Republicans, he didn't necessarily hate them—at least not all of them, and not the ones he knew personally (or the ones in his, *arghhhh*, family). But Liberal Dave knew that he could never be a Republican. His views fell squarely in the ideological space occupied by the Democratic Party.

For example, Liberal Dave completely admired the way that Democratic President Jimmy Carter had brought human rights to the forefront of American foreign policy. Liberal Dave was appalled at the treatment of Jews in what was then the Soviet Union—forbidden to practice their faith in the USSR, forbidden to leave to practice it elsewhere. Jimmy Carter had the moral clarity and courage to stand up to the Soviets and assert that some rights are universal, and there was no moral justification for using any ideology as a pretext for denying those rights. Carter's stand on human rights inspired Liberal Dave to join Amnesty International.

Of course, another famous politician of that era, Ronald Reagan, also took the Soviet Union strongly to task for its human rights record. But somehow it was cool when Carter did it but creepy when Reagan did it. Maybe it was Reagan's greasy dyed-black hair. Maybe it was that Carter was obviously an intelligent guy, and hence he must have come to his opposition to the Soviet Union after a great deal of thought; whereas Reagan obviously wasn't capable of sophisticated thought, and hence his opposition to the Soviet Union could only have been based upon superstition, chauvinism, jingoism and blind ideology. Reagan, after all, was an anti-communist, a label that had a bad connotation in Liberal Dave's mind. Liberal Dave supposed that it was acceptable to oppose communism, as President Carter was doing, as long as one wasn't an "anti-communist." The phrase "anti-communist" was almost necessarily preceded, in Liberal Dave's mind, with the phrase "knee-jerk." "Knee-jerk" meant that one had come to one's position without thinking. In the public discourse that Liberal Dave had been exposed to, anti-communists were almost always "knee-jerk anti-communists"; communists were simply communists. Anti-communism was the McCarthy hearings. It was brilliant intellectuals having their lives destroyed by know-nothing right-wing demagogues. It was the Vietnam War.

The stereotypical anti-communist (although Liberal Dave might not have perceived it as a stereotype) espoused a patriotism that was belligerent and offensive. War protesters were derided as "Commies" and "Pinkos" and greeted with slogans like "America, Love It or Leave It!" Liberal Dave knew about these patriotic bullies because he watched "All in the Family." People like Archie Bunker gave patriotism a bad name, made it a dirty word. Liberal Dave assumed that America had plenty of Archie Bunkers, except without the lovability that the show's creators had written into Archie—which they undoubtedly had to do in order to make him a sufficiently appealing character for prime time television.

If the anti-communists were bad, then those who had become the targets of their ire—at least those targets who were a part of American society—must have been good. The anti-war protestors, the hippies and the radicals who were despised by the "Love It or Leave It" crowd were remaking the popular culture into something exciting and intoxicating. If the protestors were sometimes violent, it was because they were viciously attacked by the police. If the protestors sometimes initiated the violence, it was because they were so passionate about the immorality and injustice that they were fighting valiantly to oppose; it was because they were so right and the people they were fighting were so wrong. The protests faded after Saigon fell in 1975, but much of America's youth remained under the spell of Sixties counterculture.

While Liberal Dave was anti-anti-communist, he was not pro-communist. He recognized that virtually every regime that purported to practice communism—ranging from the Soviet Union and the People's Republic of China to North Korea, Cuba and Cambodia—was a brutal, repressive dictatorship. Had time travel been possible, ConservaDave might have visited from the future and suggested to Liberal Dave that his anti-anti-communism was muddled thinking, given that communism deserved to be opposed. Even if you deducted style points from the anti-communists for being uncool, at the end of the day they were still right.

Liberal Dave would probably have dismissed that as a typical right-wing oversimplification. Liberal Dave would have indignantly insisted that his views were not muddled, but rather were *nuanced*, and that thinking liberals, unlike conservatives, had minds that could *handle complexity*. Liberal Dave was not like some non-thinking right-winger who would simply say "Communism is bad," period end of sentence. As a liberal, Liberal Dave knew that things were never black and white. He knew that one should approach a complicated issue like communism not with an arrogant and false sense of certainty and superiority, but with conflicted feelings and mixed emotions. On the one hand, communist dictatorships were brutally suppressive. On the other hand, had we not also brutally suppressed the rights of blacks, Native Americans and others? On the one hand, communist regimes had restricted freedom. On the other hand, what good is freedom when people lack food, shelter and other basic necessities? On the one hand, communist regimes were not democratic. On the other hand, who were we to impose our democratic ideals (which we didn't always live up to, by the way) on others? Liberal Dave could go back and forth like this all day, in what he probably would believe to be a *virtuoso* display of fair-mindedness. ConservaDave might have snarkily suggested that deep down, Liberal Dave believed that any idea that could be expressed without hand-wringing wasn't worth expressing.

Some of Liberal Dave's "conflicted feelings and mixed emotions" about communism probably stemmed from the ideology's utopian appeal. *Imagine no possessions/I wonder if you can/No need for greed or hunger/A brotherhood of man/Imagine all the people/Sharing all the world/You may say that I'm a dreamer/But I'm not the only one/I hope someday you'll join us/And the world will live as one.*[5] Who could possibly listen to John Lennon's ballad "Imagine" and *not* be swept away by the song's sheer idealism and beauty? Although the communist message of "Imagine" is fairly blatant, the song has never been marginalized as a communist song. Given the song's prominence in the popular culture, it's surprising how rarely the specific substance of its lyrics is ever discussed. "Imagine" has become a sort of soundtrack for idealism in general, and millions have undoubtedly sung along to it without realizing that they might as well have been singing along to *The Communist Manifesto*. Not that there's anything wrong with that….

Perhaps communism was impractical, but who could argue with a utopian ideal in which everyone's basic needs, such as food, clothing, and health care were guaranteed, in which worker's rights were protected, in which extreme poverty was eliminated? In theory, what's not to like? (ConservaDave could suggest what's not to like in theory, but the question would have Liberal Dave stumped.) And sure, all of the regimes that identified themselves as communist had fallen far short of communism's utopian ideal, but was that communism's fault? Couldn't you have a communist democracy? After all, there wasn't anything inherent in communism that required it to be paired with dictatorship, was there? *Was there?* (ConservaDave might begin his response to that question with "Well, since you asked….," but we can save the rest of the response for ConservaDave's chapter.)

The point is not that Liberal Dave wanted a communist democracy for the United States. He didn't. It's just that his objections to the idea of a communist democracy would have been more on practical grounds than on moral grounds.

All of this talk of communism might seem a little quaint, but Liberal Dave's hey day was before Reagan consigned communism to the ash heap of history. And while the overwhelming majority of Americans, including Liberal Dave, opposed communism, the way in which one expressed one's opposition to communism was often a fairly good indicator of where one stood on the political spectrum.

Liberal Dave believed that there were several other indicators of where he stood on the political spectrum. Liberal Dave instinctively rooted for the underdog (although perhaps this arose less from his liberalism than from his having grown up as a Washington sports fan). Liberal Dave wanted America to live up to its billing as the "Land of Opportunity," with no one being held back because of his or her race, ethnicity, religion, gender or political views. He believed that America's diversity was its strength. Liberal Dave was concerned about poverty: he wanted America's poor to have a genuine shot at realizing the American Dream, and hence wanted poor children throughout America to have access to a good education. His concern for the downtrodden was not limited to America: he wished for people everywhere to be free from oppression, and to have the same opportunities that he wished for his fellow Americans.

Liberal Dave realized that there was nothing special about having these attitudes. Many people had them, which is why it seemed rather clichéd to express them. None of this was anything more than any self-respecting Miss America contestant would say. Liberal Dave did believe, however, that these attitudes made him a liberal, and he was proud to identify himself as such.

In many ways, Liberal Dave's mind was an array of dots that were waiting to be connected. ConservaDave would eventually come along to connect those dots.

2 THE BIRTH OF CONSERVADAVE, PART I

"Any man who is under 30, and is not a liberal, has no heart; any man who is over 30, and is not a conservative, has no brains."

This quote is commonly attributed to Winston Churchill, although close variations of it have been attributed to several others before him. I've never liked this quote. It obviously comes from the perspective of one who is over 30 and has come to appreciate, at long last, what he now believes to be the superior wisdom of conservatism. But it seems to me that a Johnny Come Lately to any philosophy, be it conservatism, liberalism or anything else, should approach those who "saw the light" before him with humility rather than contempt. If you can imagine a conversation between a new convert to any philosophy and a long-time adherent to that philosophy, the new convert should say something like this: "I now agree with your philosophy. I used to completely disagree with it, but I now believe that you were right all along and I was wrong. I was not able to appreciate your wisdom in the past, but now I do."

Instead, the quote attributed to Churchill and others seems to reflect the following perspective: "I now agree with your philosophy. I used to completely disagree with it. However, the fact that you understood the merits of this philosophy before I did is not an indication that you were wiser than me from the beginning. It is an indication that I was morally superior to you when we were younger, because otherwise you would have been as misguided as I was." I don't know if the famous quote that starts this chapter is properly attributed to Churchill, but it reflects an arrogant chutzpah that can only be described as Churchillian. (I am actually a great admirer of Churchill, who was as determined a foe of Nazism as ever there was; he had arrogant flip side, however, as evidenced by his famous dismissal of Mahatma Gandhi as a "half-naked fakir.")

Despite my objections to the quote, it is as good a way as any to foreshadow the birth of ConservaDave as I started to approach the age of, well, 30. In order to understand the birth of ConservaDave, though, it is important to understand American politics in the age of Ronald Reagan.

Liberal Dave couldn't stand Ronald Reagan; ConservaDave idolized him. Of course, when Reagan first took office, ConservaDave had not yet been born. Although the birth records that we were able to track down are somewhat sketchy, ConservaDave appears to have been conceived sometime during Reagan's presidency and, after an unusually long period of gestation and labor, was not born until after Reagan left office.

Many people make assumptions about Democrats who become Republicans—we've all heard the jokes that a Republican is a Democrat who's been mugged, or a Democrat who has received his first mortgage bill. These jokes suggest that conversions to Republicanism occur when youthful idealism succumbs to sad resignation.

I can honestly say that was not the case with me. My own journey to the right is an example of how conservative principles can speak to the idealism even of those who were raised to believe that liberals had a monopoly on idealism.

I suggested at the end of Chapter 1 that Liberal Dave's mind was like an array of dots that were waiting to be connected. Some of these dots were actual events or experiences, some were thoughts (or merely fragments of thoughts), some were attitudes, some were preferences. In this chapter, I'll discuss some additional dots that were added to the array in the 1980s. Some of these dots were newsworthy events; most were not. What they all had in common is that they were things—events, thoughts, impressions, whatever— that happened to stick in my mind for reasons that were not necessarily clear to me at the time. In retrospect, however, all of these dots served as markers which helped lay the foundation for the birth of ConservaDave.

Dot No. 1: Reasonable People Can Disagree. I entered law school when Reagan was still in the White House. As a first year law student, I learned a phrase that has been one of my favorite expressions ever since: "Reasonable people can disagree." Actually, I wasn't taught that phrase as a simple, absolute, declarative statement. It was wrapped into a legal standard, the explanation of which would probably sound convoluted to anyone who hasn't attended law school. The specific context from which I extracted the phrase, however, is not important. What *is* important is that the phrase got me thinking that reasonable people can indeed disagree, at least on most things. That may seem obvious to most people, but it was an important lesson for a cocksure young law student named Liberal Dave who had a tendency to question the wisdom, the morality, and indeed the coolness of anyone who did not share his political views. The phrase "reasonable people can disagree" did not revolutionize my thinking overnight, but it definitely planted a seed that would eventually enable me to treat opposing points of view with more respect. As I would ultimately learn, respecting those with differing views can be dangerous: you never know where it may lead.

Dot No. 2: Warmongers! In the 1970s, the Soviet Union began deploying SS-20 missiles into Eastern Europe. The intermediate range missiles gave the Soviet Union the ability to launch nuclear attacks against the major population centers of Western Europe;

NATO had no weapons to match the SS-20's range and accuracy.[6] To meet this new Soviet threat, NATO planned to deploy a new generation of missiles—Pershing II ballistic missiles and tomahawk cruise missiles—in Western Europe. The plan to place the new NATO missiles in Western Europe was developed during the Carter Administration. However, NATO was not scheduled to deploy the new missiles until the early 1980s, by which time Reagan had become President. As the scheduled deployment of the NATO missiles neared, massive protests broke out all across Western Europe. For the protestors, Reagan came to symbolize a perceived new "cowboy" mentality in the U.S. This mentality, in the minds of the protestors, threatened to lead Europe into a nuclear war. The protestors wanted to halt NATO's deployment of the Pershing II and cruise missiles at all costs, and Reagan was their bogeyman.

Around that time, I saw an editorial cartoon. I don't remember where I saw it or who the cartoonist was, but it went something like this: In the first frame, a man labeled as "Europe" is staring passively at the reader. In the next frame, then-Soviet leader Yuri Andropov wheels up a bunch of SS-20 missiles next to "Europe Man," and leaves the missiles pointing at "Europe Man" from the East. "Europe Man" turns his head and looks nonchalantly at the Soviet missiles, and then returns to passively staring forward. In the next frame, Reagan wheels in a bunch of Pershing II missiles from the West and leaves them pointing at the SS-20s. "Europe Man" turns to see the Pershing II missiles, and then points angrily at Reagan and screams: "Warmonger!"

Dot No. 3: Give Peace a Chance, No Matter What. I was living and working in New York after finishing my undergraduate studies at Penn. The angry protests against NATO's planned deployment of missiles in Western Europe had spread to the U.S. Protestors in America had joined their brethren across the pond in an international peace movement, calling for the U.S. and the Soviet Union to implement a mutual and verifiable freeze of nuclear weapons. Peace activists were planning to stage a huge protest in New York in support of the nuclear freeze movement.

I received a telephone call from a high school friend. He had become involved in the nuclear freeze movement and was coming up to New York to attend the rally. I had read about the Reagan Administration's objections to the proposed nuclear freeze, and wanted to get the best counterarguments. My friend was an intelligent guy, so I figured that if I played devil's advocate with him, he'd be able to provide me with some good rejoinders to some of the bellicose rhetoric that was coming from the Republicans.

So, in that spirit, I asked my friend whether the protest movement wasn't being a little one-sided by putting all of its pressure on NATO and none on the Soviets. Sure, the protestors said that they wanted both sides to freeze nuclear weapons, but what real pressure were they putting on the Soviets? It seemed from news accounts that all of the protestor's anger was directed at Western leaders, especially Ronald Reagan. He, not Yuri Andropov, was the one whose effigy was being burned in streets throughout Western Europe. There were, of course, no similar protests being held in the streets of Moscow—no dissent was tolerated there. Where, then, was the pressure on Moscow to match the pressure that the protestors in the West were putting on their own leaders?

And even if both sides could be pressured equally into adopting a freeze, weren't we just freezing the Soviets into a dominant military position in Europe? After all, their SS-20s were already in place; the NATO missiles weren't. With their superior position secure, what could possibly pressure the Soviets to negotiate back down to parity in Europe? Peace protestors burning Reagan in effigy? Wasn't a permanent military imbalance in favor of the Soviets dangerous, given how they had consistently used their military might to impose a repressive form of government on their own people—as well as on hundreds of millions of other people who lived involuntarily in the Soviet sphere of influence (if "influence" is even the proper word for control that is enforced by force)? Wasn't it dangerous to cede lopsided military superiority in Europe to a regime that had repeatedly used its military power to subjugate more and more people?

Frankly, I was surprised at how well I was able to articulate the party line of the frickin' Republicans. And as I articulated it, I was surprised at how much sense it made to me. I was eager to shut up and wait for my friend's response, so that he could bring me back to my senses and provide me with ammo for any debates that I might have with the Reaganites.

After my friend listened politely to my (equally polite) positing of concerns from the Reagan perspective, this was his response: "Well, Dave, by that logic, we wouldn't be able to have a nuclear freeze."

In other words, the Reagan logic couldn't possibly be correct because it would conflict with the pre-determined goal of having a nuclear freeze. My friend was not critically evaluating whether it would be a good idea to have a nuclear freeze under then-current conditions; he was taking it as an article of faith that a nuclear freeze would be a good thing, even if it would freeze the Soviets into an overwhelming nuclear advantage in Europe. From that starting point, he evaluated my devil's advocate arguments on the basis of whether they would advance or impede the objective of freezing nuclear weapons at then-current levels. From that perspective, he of course found the arguments that I presented to be unconvincing.

I definitely agreed with my friend that it would be a good thing to drastically reduce, or even perhaps eliminate, nuclear weapons targeting Europe. What I wanted him to convince me of was how that objective could be achieved by freezing Soviet nuclear superiority in Europe into place. Why would the Soviets have any incentive to simply negotiate away their position of dominance? Why would they do this if the freeze had already given them what they wanted—cancellation of NATO's plans to deploy Pershing II and cruise missiles in Europe? Would it not make more sense to bargain from a position of strength, so that some or all of NATO's new missiles could be traded away in exchange for reductions in Soviet missiles?[7] It was these questions to which I was hoping my friend could provide a logical answer. But alas, no such logical answer was forthcoming.

In many ways, I envied my friend for being part of the protest movement, an international brotherhood and sisterhood of young people from around the world who were inspired to take to the streets and fight for something they believed in. The romance was on their side. The excitement was on their side. Could it be, though, that logic was on Reagan's side? Could it be?

I skipped the protest.

Dot No. 4: Evil Empire. On March 8, 1983, Ronald Reagan gave one of the most famous speeches of his presidency. It included the following passage:

> [I]f history teaches anything, it teaches that simple-minded appeasement or wishful thinking about our adversaries is folly. It means the betrayal of our past, the squandering of our freedom.
>
> So, I urge you to speak out against those who would place the United States in a position of military and moral inferiority....[I]n your discussions of the nuclear freeze proposals, I urge you to beware the temptation of pride -- the temptation of blithely declaring yourselves above it all and label both sides equally at fault, to ignore the facts of history and the aggressive impulses of an evil empire, to simply call the arms race a giant misunderstanding and thereby remove yourself from the struggle between right and wrong and good and evil.[8]

This speech became known as Reagan's "Evil Empire" speech, in honor of the phrase that leapt off of the text and onto headlines around the world. Reaction to the speech was swift and harsh. *New York Times* columnist Anthony Lewis called the speech "primitive" and asked: "What is the world to think when the greatest of powers is led by a man who applies to the most difficult human problem a simplistic theology?"[9] Lewis's colleague Tom Wicker called the speech "smug" and "a near-proclamation of holy war."[10] Historian Henry Steele Commager called it "the worst presidential speech in American history."[11] Reagan's speech was certainly suffused with the kind of religiosity, moral absolutism and belligerence that Liberal Dave would dismiss as typical anti-communism.

But there was other reaction, including this:

> It was the great brilliant moment when we learned that Ronald Reagan had proclaimed the Soviet Union an Evil Empire before the entire world. There was a long list of all the Western leaders who had lined up to condemn the evil Reagan for daring to call the great Soviet Union an evil empire right next to the front-page story about this dangerous, terrible man who wanted to take the world back to the dark days of the Cold War. This was the moment. It was the brightest, most glorious day. Finally a spade had been called a spade. Finally, Orwell's Newspeak was dead. President Reagan had from that moment made it impossible for anyone in the West to continue closing their eyes to the real nature of the Soviet Union.

> It was one of the most important, freedom-affirming declarations, and we all instantly knew it. For us, that was the moment that really marked the end for them, and the beginning for us. The lie had been exposed and could never, ever be untold now.

This was the reaction of Jewish activist Natan Sharansky. At the time of Reagan's speech, Sharansky was wasting away in a notorious Siberian labor camp because of his opposition to the Soviet regime and his desire to emigrate to Israel.[12] I was of course not aware of Sharansky's specific reaction to Reagan's speech at the time; Sharansky was hardly in a position to share his views with the world. It was impossible, however, to hear Reagan's phrase "evil empire" without thinking of the dissidents and hundreds of millions of others living under oppression that made that characterization difficult to dispute. Even former Carter Administration official Strobe Talbott, who had harshly criticized the "Evil Empire" speech, granted Reagan this: "He may have been impolitic, but he was not wrong."[13]

Soviet dissidents such as Sharanksy, Andrei Sakharov, Yelena Bonner, Yuri Orlov, Alexander Ginzburg and scores of others were moral giants. Many were highly accomplished in science or the arts and had, in fighting for freedoms that were taken for granted in the West, traded their relatively comfortable lives for enslavement in Siberian labor camps. *New York Times* columnists like Anthony Lewis and Tom Wicker had access to the international media, through which they could express their disgust with Reagan's speech. The dissidents incarcerated deep inside Siberia did not have that luxury. It was impossible at the time for us to hear directly from the dissidents whether they agreed that the Soviet Union was an evil empire. But how could they not agree? And how, if they were aware of the speech, could they not be cheered by an American leader who had, perhaps unfashionably, spoken truth to the power that was enslaving them?

I found myself, in spite of Liberal Dave's instincts, feeling happy that Reagan had (as Sharansky would later put it) called a spade a spade. I was happy at the thought that Reagan had invigorated the good guys—the dissidents who had the guts and character to sacrifice their freedom and risk their lives in a seemingly hopeless struggle of wills with a ruthless, all-powerful state. I compared the moral authority of the dissidents with that of the media pundits who, from the cushy comfort of the West, had managed to work themselves into a fury over Reagan's tone but were unable to lay a glove on his substance. Needless to say, I was more compelled by the courage of the dissidents than by the vanity of pundits who found it easier to hate Reagan than the oppressive system that he opposed.

In my mind, the anti-anti-communism that Liberal Dave had stubbornly adhered to was starting to collapse (like communism?) under the weight of its own logical inconsistency. How could I support the heroic dissidents if I could not countenance direct, full-throated expressions of opposition to the system that was oppressing them? I couldn't.

At the time, it was a bit of a challenge to assimilate all of the new "dots" that were appearing in my head and reconcile them with my long-held attitudes. Now, with the benefit of hindsight and perspective, I can look back and connect the dots as follows: Like many liberals, I had originally viewed Reagan's spirited challenge to communism with disdain. Most liberals (unlike hardcore leftists) were not fans of communism but, judging from our rhetoric at the time, many of us seemed to view Reagan's assertive championing of freedom, democracy and free markets as a greater threat to the world than communism. Perhaps we didn't really believe this deep down in our hearts, but how then can one explain the fact that so many of us at the time expressed our dislike for Reagan with so much more intensity and passion than we could ever muster in expressing our disapproval of brutal communist dictatorships? It was as if the liberals of America and Western Europe had unleashed so much vitriol against Reagan that we had none left for the leaders of the Soviet Union. But did this lack of balance make us appear a little too tolerant of a system which, in its denial of political, social, and economic freedom, was clearly a negation of the human spirit? Shouldn't we, as liberals, have been the most ardent and vocal opponents of such a system? Had we become so blinded by "Reagan Derangement Syndrome" that we had lost our sense of perspective, our moral compass?

As a liberal at the time Reagan was elected, I completely get why we hated him. On a surface level, there was a cultural disconnect that is exemplified by Reagan's use of the word "evil." The word reflects a religiosity that many liberals were uncomfortable with at best and contemptuous of at worst. The word also reflects the type of a stark dichotomy—good and evil, right and wrong, black and white—that liberals naturally recoil from. Liberals like to think of themselves as complex, nuanced thinkers who are sophisticated enough to appreciate ambiguity. (In my experience, many liberals indeed deserve to be described in such lofty terms; those who make fun of the intelligence of conservatives, however, are often confused thinkers rather than the complex thinkers they fancy themselves as.) Finally and most importantly, "evil" is a judgmental word. For liberals, to be judgmental is a worse sin than, well, any actual sin. The liberal aversion to being judgmental is actually something that I usually admire, and something that has stayed with me from the days of Liberal Dave. At its best, it reflects a humility where one is not always looking for ways to feel superior to people from different backgrounds, where one does not always automatically assume that one's way of doing things is better than the way that other people do things. It reflects an openness to what one might learn from people from other cultures, with different life experience, or with different viewpoints.

At its worst, though, the liberal aversion to judgmentalism can descend into a namby pamby moral equivalence that leads to an impotent inability to declare, as David Brinkley once put it, "that anything is better than anything else." At the extreme, an inability to be judgmental is an inability to make moral distinctions, and hence is an inability to be moral.

It is ironic that Reagan brought out in many of his liberal detractors the very qualities that they despised about Reagan: They were highly judgmental of Reagan and his supporters, thinking of them as caricatures wholly lacking in the nuance and complexity that they attributed to almost everyone and everything else, and attacked them with a fervor that was damn near religious.

On a deeper level, Reagan's use of words like "evil" caused a great deal of anxiety among liberals—especially in the dangerous era of Cold War nuclear gamesmanship. The possibility that differences between the U.S. and the Soviet Union might lead to nuclear war quite rightly gave everyone pause. Whatever those differences were, they certainly were not worth destroying the world over. To assert that the Soviet Union was evil, as Reagan did, put us on a path that many found to be quite scary in the Nuclear Age. Speaking out against the supposed evil of the Soviet Union's so-called "empire" would undoubtedly exacerbate tension. What if that tension got out of control, and escalated into nuclear war? The 1983 television movie *The Day After*, depicting the aftermath of a nuclear attack on the United States, tapped into the anxiety that many in the West had about the possibility of a nuclear holocaust.

Perhaps this anxiety was what subconsciously led many to attack Reagan's premise. The Soviets were *not* evil. They had lofty goals to alleviate poverty and improve the lives of workers. Sure, they had fallen short of these goals, but that was not necessarily surprising given the constant hostility and confrontation that they had to defend against from the rich nations of the world. Why couldn't we work together in a spirit of mutual respect, rather than arrogantly asserting that we were better than they were?

If the Soviets were *not* evil, then Reagan's moral challenge to the Soviet Union was misguided. Even worse, it was dangerous and potentially deadly for us all. His arrogant, self-righteous jingoism was increasing tension between the nuclear superpowers, which was increasing the danger of nuclear war. Reagan's needless saber-rattling might get us all killed. The real threat to our safety wasn't the so-called evil of the Soviets; it was the recklessness of Reagan, a right-wing nut who was liable to plunge us into a holy war.

Perhaps for some, the notion that Reagan was worse than the Soviets was convenient self-delusion that was fueled by a justifiable fear of nuclear war. If we acknowledge evil, we have a moral obligation to confront it. That doesn't mean that we have to plunge recklessly into a catastrophic war, but it does mean that we must take a clear moral stand against the evil. Since we cannot fully control or predict the actions of our adversaries, taking such a stand can be a scary course of action. By pretending that evil is not really evil, we can pretend away our moral obligation to stand up to the evil. This is particularly tempting when the price of standing up to evil is potentially so high. By pretending away the evil, we can pretend away our own moral cowardice in failing to stand up to the evil.

The problem with pretending, of course, is that it doesn't change the truth. And there were great moral and practical consequences for ignoring the truth about the Soviet Union. The brutality of the Stalin era was well known to anyone who cared to know about it: millions (and probably tens of millions) died in the slave labor camps, millions were killed by man-made famines, millions more were executed for political purposes.[14] The human rights situation in the Soviet Union improved in the post-Stalin era, but remained at a level that any honest and self-respecting liberal should have considered abominable and unacceptable. The number of political prisoners executed by the Soviet Union from 1953 through 1991 was probably between 100,000 and 200,000, and the slave labor population was still in the millions when Reagan was in office.[15] And, of course, the Soviet Union was still a place where there was no genuine right to select political leaders, no freedom of speech, no freedom of the press, no freedom of assembly, no freedom of worship, no right to due process, no economic freedom and no freedom to leave. Can you imagine liberals of the West tolerating the infringement of any of these rights for themselves? And the Soviet Union imposed these miseries not only on the Russian people, but on hundreds of millions of other unwilling subjects of many nationalities from the various Soviet republics, from the Soviet-controlled "sovereign" nations of Eastern Europe and in Soviet client states around the world.

While the Soviet Union was working to expand its empire from the latter stages of the Stalin era on through to the 1960s and 1970s, China's Mao Zedong was competing with Stalin to become the greatest mass murderer of the 20th Century. Both had surpassed Hitler. The communist regime in China, of course, spawned its own progeny in Asia, including mass murderer Pol Pot's "Killing Fields" regime in Cambodia.

In the face of all this, it is clear that Liberal Dave and others who soft-peddled the evil of communism were being both morally and intellectually dishonest. It would have been intellectually honest to have said the following: "We recognize the brutality of the Soviet Union and other communist regimes. We recognize that Western democracies, while quite flawed and far from perfect, are morally superior to the Soviet Union. However, standing up to the Soviet Union presents too great a risk of triggering a nuclear war which could kill hundreds of millions of people. That is simply too high a price to pay. Sadly, we must make the practical compromise, at least for now, of resigning the subjects of the Soviet bloc to conditions that we would never accept for ourselves, and that no human being should have to accept. We are saddened that we are unable to do more to support the aspirations for freedom of the hundreds of millions of innocent people who are imprisoned by the communist system."

In fact, many liberals did take that type of intellectually honest approach. Many others, however, allowed the practical issue—the risk of nuclear war—to cloud the moral issue of whether

communism was evil. They assumed away the moral issue in order
to avoid having to face the practical issue. By seeing no evil, they
saw nothing that they were morally obligated to confront. They
were made greatly uncomfortable by those, such as Reagan, who
refused to back down from the moral issue. Reagan forced people
like this to face the unpleasant reality of confrontation, on the one
hand, and their own moral cowardice, on the other hand. They
blamed Reagan for putting them in that uncomfortable situation,
which is why they reserved all of their acrimony for Reagan rather
than the Soviets. They twisted their minds into somehow believing
the nonsense that Reagan was morally equivalent or even inferior to
the Soviets.

It took me a while to get to the point where I could see that this
was going on. Focusing on the plight of the Soviet dissidents helped
me to get there. Lech Walesa and the rebellious ship-workers of
Gdansk, Poland, helped as well. Trying to see the world from their
perspective helped to move me away from Liberal Dave's
perspective. And I started to become disillusioned by my fellow
liberals who, I was starting to believe, had lost their moral bearings
because of their hatred of Reagan and their fear of confronting the
Soviets. I started to become offended by their moral equivalence
during times that cried out for moral clarity. My fellow liberals were
tolerating for their fellow human beings in the Soviet bloc conditions
that they would never tolerate for themselves—and this struck me as
very un-liberal. What was even worse was that they didn't have the
self-awareness (or perhaps the self-honesty) to acknowledge that this
was what they were doing.

As I noted, some liberals opposed Reagan on grounds that were
intellectually honest. They acknowledged the moral unacceptability
of the Soviet system, but contended that Reagan's assertive
challenge to Soviet communism was simply too dangerous. Reagan
proved these people wrong. It turns out that Reagan was not the
reckless cowboy that he had simplistically been portrayed as. He

was merely determined to bargain with the Soviets from a position of strength. He correctly recognized that the Soviet system was based upon force and brutality, and that bargaining with the Soviets from a position of weakness would be disastrous. That is why he was determined to match the moves that the Soviets had already taken to place missiles in Europe. His determination to follow through on the missile deployments that had been planned during the Carter Administration, in spite of intense public pressure from the left, set the stage for an historic agreement with the Soviet Union to dramatically reduce missiles on both sides. His determination to build up American military might dragged the Soviets into a race that they could not win, and which led to their collapse much sooner than most of us could have dreamed. It turns out that Reagan was right not only about the moral imperative of opposing communism, but also about the practical issue of *how* to oppose communism.

To this day, there are those on the left who dismiss this version of history as revisionist "triumphalism." In my mind, these people are scrambling to justify why they were on the wrong side of history.

Like most liberals, I had an instinctive aversion to imposing our ways on others. I still have that aversion. However, I eventually came to see Reagan's confrontation of communism not as a tribalistic attempt to impose American values on others, but as an affirmation of universal human values. And what, after all, is more idealistic than the notion that every person, regardless of the country he or she was born in or the culture he or she was born into, has the right to be free, the right to live in a society where the government serves the people at their consent? If we tolerate the denial of freedom and voting rights to people because they happen to have been born in North Korea, is that really different from tolerating the denial of freedom and voting rights to people because they were born black? Is it not more idealistic to assert that every person, regardless of the circumstances of his or her birth, is entitled to live in a free and democratic society? And aren't those who suggest that certain people are not "ready" to govern themselves engaging in the same type of bigotry, condescension and cynicism that any idealistic liberal should find revolting?

As my knee-jerk resistance to Reagan's policies, at least in the international arena, began to wear down, it was almost as if an unconscious tape-recording in my head had begun to subtly morph: *Reagan is right wing. Reagan is right wing. Reagan is right wing. Reagan is right. Reagan is right....* Could Reagan be right? Was it possible?

Reagan was enough of an idealist and a visionary to believe that a triumph of freedom and democracy over communism was not only desirable, but possible. He was widely mocked for this belief in the ideological circles that I used to run in. But he was proven right. Reagan's idealism eventually appealed to the idealism in me, and won me over.

It took me longer to be won over to conservative principles regarding economics and the role of government in society. I had grown up believing that all Republicans were selfish rich people, and I had originally assumed that Reaganomics was nothing more than a program to serve their interests. However, new dots would eventually appear in my mind. By this time, some barriers had been broken down by the fact that I had come around to Reagan's view on the most important foreign policy issues of the day. I no longer reflexively dismissed everything coming out of any Republican's mouth.

I may not have been aware of it at the time, but my feelings about the Republican fiscal and economic agenda may have been captured by a lyric by Joan Armatrading, Liberal Dave's (and ConservaDave's) favorite singer: "I am not in love. But I'm open to persuasion."[16]

3 THE BIRTH OF CONSERVADAVE, PART II

In the last chapter, I discussed some of the "dots" that entered the array in my mind during Reagan's first term as President. When I connected the dots, I came to admire Reagan's assertive moral challenge to communism. By the end of Reagan's first term, however, that was the only part of Reagan's agenda that had won me over. In 1984, I enthusiastically supported the Democratic Presidential ticket of Walter Mondale and Geraldine Ferraro. I was still very much a Democrat, and couldn't imagine ever being anything else. In other words, I was still Liberal Dave.

However, new dots kept popping into my mind. It would take a little longer for me to connect these new dots, but connect them I eventually did. Since these dots helped to guide me through the same journey that I began to recount in the last chapter, I'll pick up the numbering from where I left off:

Dot No. 5: Crocodile Dundee. In 1986, Australian actor Paul Hogan starred in the film *Crocodile Dundee*. The film, a fish-out-of-water tale about an Australian who used his Outback smarts to survive in New York City, was a smash hit. I don't recall ever having seen the film, but I did see a television interview with Hogan at the height of the movie's popularity. Hogan was comparing attitudes in England and America. In England, he said (and I'm

37

paraphrasing here), when working-class people see someone driving a fancy car, they react with resentment and jealousy: "Who does that guy think he is?" In America, when working-class people see someone driving a fancy car, they say: "I'm going to drive a car like that one day."[17]

Now, Hogan was of course generalizing, but his remarks made me think of my own experience. My origins were, as they say, humble. But although I had never been wealthy growing up, I never really had a heartfelt resentment of the wealthy. I always envisioned myself being successful in the future. I realize that not everyone's experience is the same, but the American Dream is based upon social and class mobility, of immigrants giving up everything in their homeland on the belief and expectation that they will succeed in America—and that their children's lives will be better than their own. I have heard people on the left be dismissive of this notion, but I have seen the American Dream come true over and over again throughout my life. I got a very expensive Ivy League education thanks to financial aid, and most of my friends at Penn were fellow "financial aid babies." Many of my friends at Penn were the sons and daughters of cooks, seamstresses, factory workers and other working people; almost all of them are now successful in business, engineering, law, medicine and many other fields.

Hogan's observation was hardly novel, but it did get me thinking about the optimism for which Americans—including newly arrived Americans—have always been known. This optimism and self-confidence has undoubtedly contributed to America's economic success. It was something that Reagan celebrated and sought to embody. Many on the left derided Reagan's sunny celebration of the American spirit as hokey, but I eventually came to appreciate it. Would most of us not rather live in a society characterized by class mobility, optimism and hope than in a socially and economically rigid society characterized by resignation and resentment?

Dot No. 5: Greed is Good. Towards the end of my first year of law school, I was accepted into the M.B.A. program at the University of Pennsylvania's Wharton School. I don't even remember why I applied, but I was definitely happy (and surprised) to have been accepted. It was the only business school that I had applied to. Wharton has traditionally been considered one of the top handful of business schools in the country, if not the best. I had no intention at the time of going into business, but I thought that a Wharton M.B.A. would bolster my marketability as a lawyer and would also give me a chance to learn about things that I didn't know much about. I won't say that I was brainwashed at Wharton, but by the time I graduated, I definitely had a much better understanding of the philosophical and even moral underpinnings of capitalism. I was no longer the kid whose daily ritual was to read the entire newspaper *except* the business section. I even started to read the (gasp) *Wall Street Journal*, and I must confess that my eyes probably wandered from time to time onto that paper's infamous right-leaning opinion page.

Perhaps most importantly, however, my Wharton education gave me an appreciation of the importance of incentives. If businesses have a financial incentive to produce more of a particular product, they will respond to that incentive by producing more of that product. The incentive is communicated through the free market: If, for example, a large number of people like smart phones enough to spend their hard-earned money to buy them, businesses will realize that there's money to be made there. Businesses will therefore have an incentive produce more smart phones and, lo and behold, more smart phones will be produced. You don't need a Wharton education to figure that out—except that Liberal Dave probably did need a Wharton education to figure that out.

Although I learned about the role of incentives by studying business and economics, I would later connect that "dot" to others in a way that would profoundly affect my views on public policy in general and, ultimately, politics. The key to connecting that dot was focusing on something that should be obvious: Not only do businesses respond to incentives, but people do as well. And incentives work both ways: You can have a positive incentive to do something, or a negative incentive to not do something. There are plenty of negative incentives to avoid having children out of wedlock, for example. (Fortunately for Liberal Dave, none of those negative incentives proved strong enough to keep him from being brought into this world.) Many of those negative incentives are financial: it is generally very financially burdensome for a single mother to raise children on her own. When government provides financial support to unwed mothers, it erodes the financial incentive to avoid unwed motherhood. The result will likely be that more children will be born out of wedlock, and more of the social problems that often result from that.[18] That is not to make a value judgment and say that government should never provide financial support to unwed mothers. It is simply to recognize the common sense fact that, as the saying goes, if you subsidize something you get more of it.

The same principle that applies to struggling single mothers applies to mighty corporations as well. The international financial crisis that began in 2008 was triggered by risky home mortgage loans that were made by lenders throughout the U.S. Why were all of these banks making such risky loans? Because the government was essentially providing incentives for lenders to make these risky loans and for major financial institutions to invest in the risky loans. These government policies were well intentioned: the goal was to enable more people to own their own homes. These policies, however, had the unintended effect of shielding lenders and investors from the full consequences of their risky choices. As a result, more and more lenders and investors made risky choices until the entire financial system came to the brink of collapse. If you subsidize something you get more of it.

Dot No. 6: Affirmative Action in India. Almost every American law school has a "law review," a journal that publishes scholarly articles on the law. The staff of a law review is generally made up of students at the law school who have been selected because of their good grades, their performance in a writing competition, or both. Law review is usually the most prestigious extracurricular activity that a law student can participate in; "making law review" greatly enhances a law student's marketability in the job hunt. Needless to say, I was thrilled when I was invited to join the University of Pennsylvania Law Review.

As a new member of the law review staff, I was required to write a "note"—a scholarly article on some subject of the law. All staffers were required to write notes, but not all would get their notes published in the law review. I chose to write my note on the affirmative action system in India. Affirmative action was, as ever, a hot topic in the U.S., and India had had its own version in place for much longer than the U.S. had. Was there anything that the U.S. could learn from India's experience?

As I dove into the research, I became more and more convinced that India's experience with its brand of affirmative action was a cautionary tale for the U.S. India's practices were actually far more ambitious than American affirmative action policies. In India, strict quotas were instituted to ensure a minimum representation of certain communities in government jobs, colleges, graduate and professional schools, and even the legislature. In some parts of India, these quotas (known as "reservations") consumed almost 70 percent of slots available for admission to universities or for public jobs.[19]

I found that India's reservation policies had brought forth a number of unintended consequences. Although the policies were intended to diminish the importance of India's caste system in determining who would have access to society's benefits, they arguably had the opposite effect: they gave underprivileged castes an economic incentive to hold onto their caste identity. The process became highly political, as other communities began to lobby to have themselves classified as disadvantaged so that they, too, could benefit from reservations. In the southern state of Tamil Nadu, for example, it was estimated at one point that 80 percent of the population was eligible for reservations.[20] A reservation policy that benefits 80 percent of the population (at the expense of the other 20 percent) becomes almost impossible to scale back in a democratic society. Although reservation policies are supposedly intended to be temporary remedies to be used only as long as they're necessary, the beneficiaries of those policies never have the incentive to concede that the policies are no longer needed. When the beneficiaries of reservation policies constitute a solid majority of the population, it creates political momentum to enshrine "temporary" quotas into permanent entitlements. That, in turn, gives communities that do not benefit from reservations a strong incentive to band together and lobby to be included. This dynamic tends to solidify, rather than erode, everyone's sense of identification with their own community, and hence exacerbate, rather than alleviate, the potential for conflict among different communities.

When such a large percentage of the population benefits from quotas, one has to wonder whether all of the protected communities really need protection. Even if one believes that quotas are a good policy to help people overcome the debilitating effects of discrimination, it does not follow that quotas should apply to every minority group. India's reservation policies were originally designed to protect the victims of the most virulent discrimination, particularly those formerly known as the "untouchables." Did it really make sense to take a remedy that was originally designed to rehabilitate the very most victimized in society, and expand that remedy to apply to a majority of the society? Was that not likely the result of a political coalition-building process in which the leaders of various communities essentially said to one another: "We'll support continued quotas for you if you support quotas for us"?

India's reservation policies caused a number of other problems. They motivated many of India's best and brightest to leave the country. They encouraged corruption and abuse, with reports that officials were bribed into falsely certifying that certain people were entitled to the benefit of quotas. They benefited wealthy and well-connected members of protected communities at the expense of more disadvantaged members of communities that were not protected. The worst thing about India's reservation policies, I came to conclude, was that they reinforced the very notion that they were designed to combat: that one's opportunities in life were determined by what community one was born into. Every person was competing to share in a pre-determined slice of the pie that had been set aside for his or her community. The size of the slice was determined by an intensely political process driven almost entirely by identity politics. It seemed to me that India's reservation policies had strayed far from the idealistic vision of trying to give everyone in society an equal opportunity to succeed.

I had never been terribly offended by affirmative action in America, which has always been much more benign than the reservation policies of India. I've never believed that there was much danger that the U.S. would take affirmative action as far as India had taken its reservation policies, at least not anytime soon. Taking a close look at India's policies, however, caused me to raise many of the same concerns, in the context of India, that conservatives would raise about affirmative action in America. My law review note, in expressing skepticism about reservation policies in India, could perhaps have been interpreted as implying skepticism about affirmative action in America.

Coincidentally, during the year that I was researching and writing my note on India's reservation policies, the editorial board of Penn's law review adopted an affirmative action policy of its own. The policy essentially provided that the standards for selecting the law review staff would be relaxed to the extent necessary to ensure that a "sufficient" number of minority group members were chosen. The editorial board was clearly committed to the concept of affirmative action. It was intent on ensuring that there would be diversity on the law review staff—or at least diversity of skin color, if not diversity of thought.

I was not surprised that my note on Indian affirmative action was never published.

Dot No. 7: Secretary Kemp. On February 13, 1989, Jack Kemp was sworn in as Secretary of Housing and Urban Development in the Administration of President George H.W. Bush. At the time, I knew a little about Kemp—mostly that he was big on "supply side economics," and had talked about putting us back on the gold standard. I basically thought of him as a hard-core right-winger. And even though I wasn't really Liberal Dave any longer, "hard-core right winger" was not my idea of a compliment. I was also aware that Kemp was a former football player and, although I was a big football fan, this made him remind me of Gerald Ford—again, not my idea of a compliment (at least not at the time).

At the time, I didn't know anything about Jack Kemp's vision of "Compassionate Conservatism." That would soon change, however, as I started reading articles profiling the new HUD Secretary. Up until then, I had found nothing in the Republican economic agenda that really appealed to my idealism. That, too, would soon change.

When I started to read about what Kemp stood for, a light went off in my head. *This* is right. *This* is what I believe in. Like few political ideas that I had encountered before, Kemp's Compassionate Conservatism felt right in my heart and made sense in my head. It was as if Kemp's ideas had been brewing independently in my own mind, but I had never been able to put the pieces together until I finally discovered the work that Kemp and others had been doing for years. And when I finally put the pieces together, with their help, I was quite surprised at where those pieces fell on the political spectrum.

Kemp, Robert Woodson and others developed an agenda for a Conservative War on Poverty. They, like me, lauded the goals of the War on Poverty launched by Democratic President Lyndon Johnson in the 1960s. However, by the 1980s, it had become apparent that throwing money at the problem was not the answer. Despite billions of dollars spent on anti-poverty programs, the urban underclass was growing, not shrinking, and the social pathologies of the inner city were becoming worse, not better.

By applying conservative principles to fight poverty, people like Kemp and Woodson identified why well intentioned liberal programs were failing. And they designed a platform that, in my view, demonstrated a much higher level of idealism, and a much greater belief in human potential, than could be found in the assumptions underlying the liberal war on poverty.

In the inner city, liberal poverty programs were inadvertently exacerbating problems that arose from America's troubled racial history. By providing money and services to the poor, poverty programs were helpful in the short run. However, these programs created a sense of dependence that undermined the spirit and confidence of those that the programs were designed to help. The effect was especially damaging in largely African-American inner city communities. Johnson's War on Poverty was launched shortly after America was ending segregation in the South and was breaking down barriers to African-American political participation throughout the country. African Americans had endured centuries of hostile racism in this country, and in the 1960s, official government policies in parts of the country were still based upon the assumption that blacks were inferior to whites. (In those days, race in America was thought of almost exclusively in terms of black and white; I can attest to the fact that "browns" existed too, but the majority did not appear to discover that until later.)

Shortly after overt hostile racism was at long last mostly eliminated from official policies in this country (although not from people's hearts), the War on Poverty was launched. An unintended side effect on the War on Poverty in African-American communities was that it replaced hostile racism with condescending racism. The myth of black inferiority was reinforced in the black inner city with a subconscious message that blacks could not compete with whites without a great deal of special help. This subconscious message was also delivered inadvertently through the well-intentioned policy of racial preferences. George W. Bush would later describe the condescending racism of white liberal proponents of these programs as "the soft bigotry of low expectations."

Woodson, Kemp and like-minded conservatives did not advocate that the War on Poverty be abandoned, but rather that it be redesigned on the basis of conservative principles. At the heart of their program was a very important assumption that had somehow escaped the well-meaning white liberals who designed the original War on Poverty: Poor people are just like everyone else. Like everyone else, poor people respond to incentives. If you design programs for the poor that reward bad choices, such as having children out of wedlock, the poor will have more children out of wedlock and perpetuate the cycle of poverty. Like everyone else, poor people will make the effort to succeed if they believe that their effort will be rewarded. If you undermine a person's belief that he or she will ever be good enough to succeed, that person will be less likely to make the effort necessary to succeed. Like everyone else, poor people defend and take care of things that they have a stake in. Communities of homeowners, even if they are poor, are better equipped to fight urban social pathologies than communities in which the residents have no ownership.

In short, the liberal War on Poverty was undermined by the condescending assumption that, to twist the words of F. Scott Fitzgerald, "the poor are different."

Throughout our history, people have succeeded in America by getting educated, working hard, making good choices, claiming a stake in their society and taking responsibility for their actions. People like Kemp and Woodson reminded us that the urban poor were no different, and that they could succeed by following the same path that others had followed. African Americans had been held back by centuries of official racism, but the solution was not to segregate the black urban poor into a path that veered them away from the traditional recipe for success. Proponents of the Conservative War on Poverty did not suggest that racism was no longer an obstacle to African-American advancement. They merely suggested that racism had become, with the removal of the most heinous official barriers to advancement, a *surmountable* obstacle. They noted that black immigrants from Africa and the Caribbean, even though they came to this country poor, typically had greater success than native-born inner city blacks. This was because they approached life with the mindset, values and self-belief of immigrants, rather than the attitudes of those with an induced dependence on government help. These black immigrants faced the same racism that American-born blacks faced, but were more likely to overcome it because they believed that they could overcome it.

This Compassionate Conservative vision appealed to my idealism. At its heart was a great belief in human potential, free of the pity and condescension that undermined earlier efforts to fight poverty. I was eventually able to put my finger on what had been bugging me about the liberal War on Poverty: In an effort to spread to the poor some of the most basic material benefits of the American Dream, the liberal War on Poverty actually robbed the poor of the spirit that fueled the American Dream—the self-confidence, the self-reliance, the optimism, the daring. As such, the safety net for many became a glass ceiling, defining not only a material level below which they would not sink, but a level above which they would not rise because we had undermined the mindset necessary to climb above it. Some on the left probably devalued the spirit of the American Dream because it had not worked for everyone. That was a "glass-half-empty" view of the world. In contrast, Compassionate Conservatism took a "glass-half-full" approach: Let us celebrate the American Dream, try to understand how its magic has worked for so many, and try to figure out how to bottle that magic so that it can work for as many Americans as possible. Let us dream of a society where the poor—without being delusional—can look at the rich not with envy and resentment, but with a sense that they are envisioning the possibilities of their own future. If there are barriers to achieving that society, then let's figure out how to break down those barriers without throwing out the baby with the bathwater—without undermining the spirit that inspires people to strive for success.

There are several policies that have fallen under the ambit of Compassionate Conservatism: welfare reform and workfare, to help welfare recipients transition into the workforce; enterprise zones and empowerment zones, to help attract jobs and free enterprise into poor areas; homeownership programs, including tenant ownership of public housing units, to enable the poor to claim an ownership stake in their communities; school choice, to give parents the power of consumers of their children's education and force public schools to compete with parochial and other private schools to provide quality education; empowerment of faith-based community social service organizations that can be more effective in helping the poor than are government bureaucracies; and others. The common thread of these policies is that they are designed to promote empowerment over dependence, to incentivize productive choices over destructive choices, and to facilitate the expansion of capitalism into poor areas. Some of these policies have been very successful and some have had kinks that need to be worked out. Policies, however, can be refined and improved over time. The important thing is to get the philosophical foundation right. Once that is done, we can focus on specific practical issues that must be addressed in order for the policies to actually work. Compassionate Conservatism is not a bagful of magic policy panaceas, but rather a philosophy that can guide us to develop more effective policies.

A lot of liberals just didn't get Compassionate Conservatism. Many asserted, only half-jokingly, that the phrase itself was oxymoronic—that one couldn't be compassionate and conservative at the same time. Many liberals would no doubt be surprised to learn that conservative households give roughly 30 percent more to charity than liberal households, despite the fact that liberal households have higher incomes, and that conservatives also give more of their time to charitable activities than do liberals.[21]

In the same way that many Democrats eventually came to admire the way that Reagan stood up to communism, many Democrats have also come to accept much of the Compassionate Conservative agenda. It was President Clinton, after all, who worked with a Republican Congress to get welfare reform passed. However, the ability of many Democratic politicians to publicly support other important parts of the Compassionate Conservative agenda, such as school choice, has been impeded by their dependence on powerful special interest groups such as the teachers unions.

Although Compassionate Conservatism encompassed a fairly limited (albeit important) range of issues, it had an impact on me that went much further. It gave me a framework from which to think about other issues. It made me realize that I was, like it or not, a conservative. That didn't mean that I agreed with everything that every conservative, or even most conservatives, stood for. It just meant that that small ideological corner of the universe that I felt most comfortable in happened to be in a conservative galaxy.

With the way that Reagan had influenced my thinking on foreign policy and Kemp had now influenced my thinking on domestic policy, I no longer felt comfortable identifying myself as a Democrat. It's not as if I suddenly found Democrats in general to be morally objectionable, it's just that I was no longer one of them. But the idea of becoming a Republican was, at least at first, a tough pill to swallow for someone who had spent his entire life as Liberal Dave. What would happen if I registered as a Republican? Would my IQ drop? Would I start listening to Pat Boone? Would my Samoan lips shrink? I was filled with anxiety. But maybe good things would happen, as well. Maybe I would become rich and join the cabal that controls America.

But seriously, folks, I did have serious misgivings about becoming one of *them*. I still harbored many of Liberal Dave's prejudices. I knew, however, that I needed to be true to myself, and eventually brought myself to swallow hard and do the dirty deed. I officially registered as a Republican. At long last, ConservaDave was born.

In retrospect, actually becoming a Republican, and getting to know Republicans through political activity, was a great way for me to overcome my prejudices about Republicans. I got to know them as actual people, rather than stereotypes. Some Republicans, of course, actually fit the stereotypes that liberals have of Republicans, just as some liberals fit the stereotypes that conservatives have of liberals. Most people, I am sad to report to some of you, do not fit the stereotypes, especially when you really get to know them.

I still am not a lock-step conservative on all issues. For example, I tend to be less conservative on the social issues championed by the Religious Right. However, for those issues on which I am still Liberal Dave, I generally have an understanding of and respect for the conservative position that I had not had in my earlier days. Some of that comes from maturity, but most of it comes from having now had the opportunity to discuss these issues with my fellow conservatives in a spirit of mutual respect. I have now seen that positions that Liberal Dave would have found repugnant are held by people whose intelligence and good will cannot be questioned—at least not by me. And I have listened generously so that I now appreciate the logic behind these positions, even in those cases where I still am not ultimately convinced by that logic.

When I try to explain my conservative idealism to my liberal friends, some will respond with a long litany of rotten things that Republicans have allegedly done. If I wanted to, I could respond with an equally long litany of rotten things that Democrats have done. But that would miss the point. Partisans on both sides tend to have a highly biased recollection of who did what to whom, and seem to have a psychological need to believe that their side is as pure as the driven snow. To paraphrase my grandmother, partisans on both sides are blissfully oblivious to the odor of their own feces. As a Republican, I should not be expected to vouch for everything that every Republican has ever done, just as Democrats should not be expected to vouch for everything that every Democrat has ever done.

Since becoming ConservaDave, I have found kindred spirits on both the left and the right. I have also found many spirits, on both the left and the right, who are not so kindred. I have come to the conclusion that people can gravitate to the left or to the right for good reasons or bad reasons. You can be liberal because you think it makes you *appear* to be a good person. You can be liberal because you have genuine empathy for the least fortunate in society. You can be conservative because your religion teaches you to help the least fortunate in society. You can be conservative because you want to impose your religion on the rest of society. You can be liberal because you feel the need to be liked by the "world community." You can be conservative because you think the opinion of the "world community" does not matter at all. You can be liberal because you don't understand economics. You can be conservative because you do understand economics and are using that understanding to further your personal greed. You can be liberal because you rely on emotion to the exclusion of reason. You can be conservative because you rely on reason to the exclusion of emotion.

You can be liberal because you are idealistic, fair and passionate about making society better. You can be conservative for the same reasons. I like to think that I'm on the right for the right reasons, and I respect people who are on the left for the right reasons. There are many brands of conservatism, just as there are many brands of liberalism. The brand of conservatism that I subscribe to is hopeful, youthful and idealistic.

So, now that ConservaDave had come into this world, what had become of Liberal Dave? Recall that at the end of the first chapter, I listed a series of Liberal Dave's beliefs as he might have expressed them had he been a Miss America contestant. Let's go through Liberal Dave's "Miss America speech" point by point and check off the views that ConservaDave would agree with:

Liberal Dave instinctively rooted for the underdog. CHECK.

Liberal Dave wanted America to live up to its billing as the "Land of Opportunity," with no one being held back because of his or her race, ethnicity, religion, gender or political views. CHECK.

He believed that America's diversity was its strength. CHECK.

Liberal Dave was concerned about poverty: he wanted America's poor to have a genuine shot at realizing the American Dream, and hence wanted poor children throughout America to have access to a good education. CHECK.

His concern for the downtrodden was not limited to America: he wished for people everywhere to be free from oppression, and to have the same opportunities that he wished for his fellow Americans. CHECK.

So, clearly, Liberal Dave continued to live on in the body, heart and mind of ConservaDave. But this was not some bad science fiction experiment gone awry, as in Steve Martin's movie *The Man with Two Brains*. This was a demonstration that there was actually much common ground shared by Liberal Dave and ConservaDave (and Miss America!). Was there hope for the world after all?

4 LEFT-HEARTED, RIGHT-MINDED

On April 15, 2009, CNN correspondent Susan Roesgen found herself trapped behind enemy lines. Roesgen wasn't covering the war in Iraq or Afghanistan; she was covering a Chicago "Tea Party" protest against excessive government spending. Given how Roesgen was so clearly culturally alienated from thousands of protestors that surrounded her that day, she might as well have been covering a Taliban rally. Poor Susan was a lone Liberal Dave in a sea of ConservaDaves, and clearly wasn't comfortable.

Roesgen had covered protests for CNN before. In 2006, she covered a protest in New Orleans demanding more federal money to repair levees damaged by Hurricane Katrina. The protest took place while President George W. Bush was visiting New Orleans. One protestor was wearing a George W. Bush mask—that is, George W. Bush with Satan's horns and Hitler's mustache. "Bush/Satan/Hitler" was waving around a wad of play money, perhaps to symbolize Republican greed or something of the sort. Roesgen reported that the protest organizers "hoped the President would stop by after his meeting with business leaders." The camera then zoomed in on the masked demonstrator as Roesgen's narration continued: "But while a look-alike showed up with a wad of cash, Mr. Bush did not."

Roesgen did not seem particularly perturbed that a demonstrator would compare Bush not only to Hitler (that was old hat by then) but to Satan as well. The masked protestor whom Roesgen so casually referred to as a Bush "look-alike" was presented as an amusing prop in a piece sympathetic to the demonstrators.[22]

Roesgen rediscovered her sense of moral outrage, though, when it came time to cover the Tea Party. She confronted a protestor holding a sign depicting President Obama as Hitler. Angrily pointing at the sign, Roesgen demanded: "What is this supposed to mean? What do you mean by that?"

"Well, I mean he's a fascist," said the man. "The pirates—"

"Wait! Why do you say he's a fascist? He's the President of the United States," Roesgen cut in.

"He *is* a fascist," insisted the demonstrator.

"Do you realize how—do you realize how *offensive* that is?" demanded Roesgen, no doubt finally realizing at that moment that it was also offensive to compare President Bush to both Hitler *and* Satan—or maybe not. Roesgen and the demonstrator continued their pointless back and forth, with Roesgen repeatedly demanding to know *why* President Obama was a fascist and the demonstrator simply insisting that Obama *was* a fascist. Roesgen's attempt to interview her hand-pick loon with the Obama-as-Hitler sign was about as enlightening as it would have been for her to interview any of the countless loons with Bush-as-Hitler signs that used to show up at anti-war rallies—except we can't know for sure because journalists like Roesgen never highlight or challenge the extremist loons at left-wing rallies.

At one point, the Tea Party protestor told Roesgen that we need term limits. But Roesgen promptly steered the conversation back to the riveting "Is *not*! Is *too*!" battle the two had been locked in before: "Why be so hard on the President of the United States though with such an *offensive* message?"

After the protestor responded by insisting yet again that Obama is a fascist, Roesgen mercifully ended the conversation with a sarcastic "okaaaaaay."

Roesgen then moved on to accost her next victim, a man holding his two-year-old son. Roesgen asked the man why he was attending the rally, and he responded: "Because I hear a President say that he believed in what Lincoln stood for," the man started. "Lincoln's primary thing was he believed that people had the right to liberty and they had the right—"

"Sir, what does this have to do with taxes?" Roesgen angrily cut in. "What does this have to do with your taxes? Do you realize that you're eligible for a $400 credit—"

"Let me finish my point," said the man. "Lincoln believed that people had the right to share in the fruits of their own labor and that government should not take it. And we have clearly gotten to that point—"

"Wait," Roesgen again cut in. "Did you know that the state of Lincoln gets $50 billion out of this stimulus? That's $50 billion for this state, Sir." Roesgen clearly thought that she had shown what a fool this man was for protesting Obama, when Obama's stimulus plan would supposedly provide him with a $400 tax credit and $50 billion for his state.

It was completely lost on Roesgen that this was precisely the kind of reckless government largesse that the Tea Partiers were protesting, and they didn't care that the spending was supposedly "for their own good." Their concern was that out-of-control government spending was building up a massive debt that would place an unconscionable burden on that man's two-year-old son and others of his generation. Roesgen, no doubt, viewed the whole thing through the lens of traditional liberal coalition politics: "Blacks, here's something for you; and Jews, here's something for you; and Hispanics, here's something for you; and unions, here's something for you; and...." Roesgen could not comprehend why anyone would not rejoice at the prospect of the federal government providing "something for them." It clearly had never occurred to her that potential recipients of government goodies might be concerned about how those goodies would be paid for. A tax credit for you and $50 billion for your state? What kind of idiot would be against that?

Apparently satisfied that she had just laid the man and his two-year-old son to waste, Roesgen didn't even wait for the man's reply. She stepped away and addressed the camera: "I think you get the general tenor of this," said Roesgen who, before signing off, made sure to take a gratuitous shot at "the right-wing conservative network Fox." Welcome to the Tea Party, Susan Roesgen.[23]

The Tea Party movement was inspired by CNBC reporter Rick Santelli's on-air rant from a Chicago trading floor on February 19, 2009, in which he decried the Obama Administration's plan for taxpayers to bail out homeowners who could not pay their mortgages. Santelli complained that "the government is promoting bad behavior" by protecting people from the consequences of their decisions to buy homes that were beyond their means. At one point, Santelli turned to the traders behind him on the floor and shouted: "How many of you people want to pay for your neighbor's mortgage that has an extra bathroom and can't pay their bills?" As the crowd booed supportively, Santelli turned back to the camera and asked: "President Obama, are you listening?" Near the end of his self-described rant, Santelli called for a "Chicago Tea Party" in support of capitalism.[24] By April 15, 2009—Tax Day—a grass roots movement had come together to stage demonstrations not only in Chicago, but in cities all over the country.

To be fair, Susan Roesgen was hardly the only member of the mainstream media that didn't know what to make of the Tea Party movement. Roesgen's CNN colleague Anderson Cooper and many other mainstream journalists took to calling the protestors "teabaggers." The *Urban Dictionary* defines "teabagger" as "a man that dips [certain intimate parts of his anatomy] into the mouth of another person (as if dipping a tea bag into hot water)."[25] (ConservaDave had never heard of that term. Liberal Dave, of course, was more up to date on his modern slang.) Lest anyone give Cooper the benefit of the doubt that his reference to "teabagging" was innocent, consider this on-air exchange with David Gergen on April 15, 2009:

> GERGEN: Republicans have got a way—They still haven't found their voice, Anderson. They're still— this happens to a minority party after they've lost a couple of bad elections, but they're searching for their voice.
>
> COOPER *(with a smirk)*: It's hard to talk when you're teabagging.
>
> *[Gergen and Ali Velshi giggle.]*[26]

Not to be outdone, MSNBC's David Shuster unleashed this *tour de force* of comic genius and incisive commentary:

> For most Americans, Wednesday, April 15, will be Tax Day, but . . . it's going to be Teabagging Day for the right wing, and they're going nuts for it. Thousands of them whipped out the festivities early this past weekend, and while the parties are officially toothless, the teabaggers are full-throated about their goals. They want to give President Obama a strong tongue-lashing and lick government spending….That's "teabagging" in a nutshell.[27]

Liberal Dave almost bust a gut a laughing, thinking with disdain about all those stupid conservatives *who don't even know what teabagging means. We're laughing at them, and those conservative idiots don't even know why.* Shuster was so *naughty*—so *subversive!* And after all, nothing signifies one's moral and intellectual superiority like knowing a slang term for an obscure sex act that the other guy doesn't know.

ConservaDave watched the same report, but was not as impressed with Shuster's attempt at humor. A little too junior high school for his taste. And plus, ConservaDave thought the "Teabaggers" were making important points. At the dawn of the Tea Party movement, taxpayers were spending hundreds of billions of dollars to bail out the financial services industry and the car companies. The bailouts had started under President Bush and were expanding under President Obama, who had also recently signed a $787 billion stimulus bill (the estimated cost was later raised to $830 billion[28]) in an effort to revive the economy. The Tea Party was raising important questions: How are we going to pay for all of this? Is it fair to amass such an unprecedented debt burden and pass it on to our children? Will the rapid expansion of the size and role of government infringe upon our free market economy? How will it affect our liberty? Will we eventually collapse under the weight of a welfare state that we can't afford? And the fight over Obamacare, which would add the first major federal entitlement program since 1965 and greatly increase government's role in health care, had not yet even begun.

The Tea Partiers would continue to be maligned, characterized by the mainstream media and liberal politicians as racists, terrorists and extremists. Now to be sure, there were racists and extremists among the ranks of the Tea Party—every movement attracts a fringe element. Anyone who would compare Barack Obama to Hitler is just as much of a hateful nut job as, well, anyone who would compare George W. Bush to Hitler. But the mainstream media never paints leftist protest movements in the image of their most extreme followers. Had the Tea Party's critics applied the same standards to those leftist protest movements as they did to the Tea Party, then the Iraq War protestors would have been dismissed as extremists who were filled with hatred not only for President Bush, but for America; the Wisconsin public sector union protestors of 2011 would have been characterized by their hateful, violent rhetoric and unruly behavior; and the Occupy Wall Street movement would have been painted as a violent collection of socialists, communists and anti-Semites who had America's worst enemies cheering.

Why was the Tea Party singled out for such vitriol? Perhaps because it was the bearer of bad news to liberals: their agenda, as we had come to know it, was no longer a viable option because we could no longer afford it. The Tea Party virtually willed America's debt problem onto the national agenda. Their activism got average Americans to understand that we simply couldn't afford for government to continue to spend and accumulate debt at the rate that it was doing. The debt problem is an existential threat to the agenda of many on the left—namely, to move America closer to the model of the European welfare state. That agenda requires expanding the federal welfare state by adding entitlement programs. But how can we do that if our debt problem leaves us unable to afford the entitlement programs that we already have?

The Tea Partiers didn't create the debt problem; they simply helped the majority of Americans to see that the problem existed, and made it impossible for politicians of either party to ignore it. For some liberals, it was like telling them that there was no Santa Claus.

Perhaps all the name-calling against the Tea Party was an attempt to avoid dealing with the Tea Party's message: the era of big government is over—for real, this time.

It was of course President Clinton who famously declared in 1996 that "the era of big government is over."[29] Clinton held up his end of the bargain: Helped by a buoyant dot.com economy and a Republican Congress, the national debt increased only modestly to $5.7 trillion after Clinton's two terms. The debt almost doubled to $10.6 trillion, however, after eight years of President George W. Bush, and shot up to over $15 trillion in just the first three years of

Obama's presidency. Debt in the Obama Administration increased more than twice as fast as it did under Bush, who in turn ran up the debt about twice as fast as Clinton did.[30]

Folks like Liberal Dave love to cite a quote attributed to former Vice President Dick Cheney: "Reagan proved that deficits don't matter." Former Treasury Secretary Paul O'Neill claims that Cheney said that to him back in 2002. [31] Liberals often invoke that quote to show that Republicans are hypocrites who only care about deficits when the Democrats are in power. (A deficit occurs when the government spends more than it takes in during a fiscal year, which runs from October 1 through September 30; the government has to borrow that amount, and hence it gets added to the debt which accumulates over time.)

Cheney's quote, however, is hardly a liberal trump card. The national debt has more than doubled since Cheney allegedly made the statement back in 2002, and has increased by more than five times since Reagan left office.[32] The federal deficit for 2002 was $159 billion;[33] it was almost nine times higher, $1.4 trillion, in 2009.[34] When Cheney supposedly said that deficits don't matter, we were adding to a relatively manageable debt with deficits that paled in comparison to the trillion-dollar-plus deficits that have become the new normal.

Reasonable people can disagree on whether deficits mattered back then. They certainly matter now. By 2011, the national debt had exploded to a record $15 trillion[35]—greater than the combined value of all of the goods and services produced in our entire economy during the previous year.[36] Carrying such an enormous debt is placing a tremendous burden on all of us and an even greater burden on our children and grandchildren.

Consider that we had to pay more than $200 billion in 2011 just to cover the interest on our debt—almost as much as we spent on medical services to the poor under Medicaid. We're on a path to almost quadruple our annual interest bill over the next 10 years, to the point where interest payments would be 17% more than our Medicare budget for senior citizen health care and 82% more than all non-security spending   combined (other than entitlements like Medicare, Medicaid and Social Security).[37] The interest on our debt is like an insatiable monster that keeps gobbling up more and more of our funds—funds we'd rather spend on things like national security, infrastructure and programs to help the poor and elderly.

Much of the interest on our debt goes straight overseas. Foreigners hold about 47 percent of our publicly held debt[38] and China owns the largest chunk of that.[39]

There's a very real risk that the cost of our debt could skyrocket, even well beyond the scary projections just mentioned. That would result in our interest payments sucking off an even greater share of our public funds, severely hindering the federal government's ability to properly fund defense, infrastructure and everything else— including all the social programs that liberals champion.

What might cause the interest rates on our debt to spike well above the levels that are currently projected?   America has traditionally been able to borrow money at fairly low rates of interest.   The U.S. borrows by selling Treasury securities— essentially IOUs where Uncle Sam agrees to repay the principal, plus interest, on specified due dates.   Treasuries are bought by various types of investors, such as individuals, banks, pension funds, businesses and foreign central banks.   Treasury securities have traditionally been considered one of the very safest investments out there, because it has been inconceivable that the U.S. government would fail to repay its obligations when due.   For that and other reasons, there has always been a very strong demand for Treasury securities and investors have always been willing to buy them (either directly from the U.S. government or from other investors) at low interest rates.

America received a jolt in 2011 when, for the first time in history, the U.S. credit rating was downgraded by a major credit rating agency. Investors generally look to the major credit rating agencies—Standard & Poor's (which is particularly influential in rating the debt of countries), Moody's Investor Service and Fitch Ratings—for guidance on which investments are safer than others. Prior to August 5, 2011, when Standard & Poor's lowered the U.S. credit rating from AAA to AA+, U.S. debt had always held the highest possible rating from each of the "Big Three" credit rating agencies.[40]   Just as banks charge people with lower credit scores higher interest on their loans in order to compensate them for the greater risk of not getting repaid, investors generally demand higher interest rates to induce them to invest in the debt of countries with lower credit ratings.

The immediate effect of the Standard & Poor's downgrade was not as dramatic as it could have been, but there is reason to believe that there may be a delayed reaction. The downgrade did not immediately tank demand for Treasury securities for several reasons. Given the recent instability in international financial markets, there was no clear alternative to replace U.S. Treasuries as the safe investment of choice. That could eventually change, especially if we lag behind other countries in confronting our fiscal problems.

Also, much of the demand for Treasuries exists because the U.S. Dollar remains the dominant currency of choice for international transactions—even transactions that don't involve U.S. parties. Foreign businesses and central banks need to have dollar-denominated investments such as U.S. Treasuries in order to participate in the international economy.   However, many economists expect a rapid rise in the number of international transactions that will use the currencies of Europe or China rather than the dollar.[41] If other currencies grab a significant share of international transactions, then demand for the dollar will drop, demand for U.S. Treasuries will drop, and Uncle Sam will have to offer higher interest rates in order to entice investors to continue to buy Treasuries.

Another scenario that scares international investors is that the U.S. might deal with its crushing debt burden by simply creating more dollars with which to pay its debt obligations. The U.S. can create more dollars either by actually printing them, or through the Federal Reserve buying assets from its member banks.[42] These are traditional means of controlling the money supply, which affects prices, the availability of credit and other important elements of the economy. It sounds like we have a magic formula where we can simply create money and use it to repay our debt—but there's a major catch. The more dollars we create, the less each dollar is worth. The European investor who owns Treasuries gets income in dollars, which he then has to convert to euros in order buy things in his home country. When those dollars become worth less, he'll get fewer euros when he converts them and he won't be a happy camper. He and his fellow investors around the world will then demand higher interest rates in order to continue lending the federal government money (i.e. buying Treasuries).

If the interest that we have to pay on Treasuries shoots up for any of these or other reasons, then the projection that we'll have to pay $928 billion[43] per year in interest by 2020 or so—staggering as that amount is—could be laughably optimistic. Under that scenario, it is difficult to imagine how the federal government could come close to funding the range of activities that it funds today. The question will not be whether we will drastically cut government programs—we will. The question will be whether the terms of our scale-back of government will be dictated to us by crisis, or whether we will choose our own terms by making difficult decisions in time to avert catastrophe.

Some people seem to think that we could continue to have as big a government as we want, and continue to add to the list of entitlement programs, if only we would sufficiently tax the "rich." That simply isn't possible. Even if we taxed *100 percent* of the income of all of the millionaires and billionaires, we still wouldn't come close to covering the budget deficit.[44] And punitive taxation of the rich (even short of 100 percent!) would severely dampen the ability and incentive of those people to make the investments we need to create jobs. If people with the ability to invest have less money to invest—and if we reduce, through higher taxes, the potential rewards for them to risk the money they have left—they will invest less in our economy. The economy will generate fewer jobs and less wealth, which means that the government will have less revenue to fund essential (and not-so-essential) programs and services. Government might try to create public sector jobs to take up the slack, but those jobs cannot be sustained without revenues from a productive private sector.

We simply cannot correct the disastrous course that we're on without reforming entitlements—those programs, such as Medicare, Medicaid and Social Security, where qualifying individuals are legally entitled to receive benefits regardless of the total cost. Social Security, Medicare and Medicaid make up 46 percent of the federal budget.[45] Social Security and Medicare are projected to grow significantly—with people living longer and Baby Boomers entering retirement age, senior citizens are increasing in number. Adding in other entitlement programs, interest on the debt and other required spending, total mandatory spending swallows up over 60 percent of the budget—and will continue to swallow up more if entitlement programs aren't reformed. Defense accounts for 20 percent of the budget, and *everything else* makes up only 19 percent. The federal budget is thus dominated by entitlements, the outlays for which are rapidly increasing on autopilot. And we are now instituting a major new entitlement called "Obamacare."

The first problem with entitlements is that they're impossible to control unless they're reformed or abolished. The second problem with entitlements is that they're almost impossible to reform or abolish. Once people get used to the idea that they're "entitled" to certain benefits from the government, trying to tell them otherwise becomes an electoral death wish for politicians. And, since politicians are the ones that we have to rely upon to reform entitlements….Well, you get the picture.

We're on a completely unsustainable path where our children and grandchildren will have to borrow large sums of money *just to pay the interest* on the large sums of money that we're borrowing today to spend on ourselves. We're setting up a huge intergenerational transfer of wealth in the wrong direction. Rather than passing our wealth on to our children and grandchildren so that their lives can be better than ours, we're passing our debts onto them to a degree that will cripple their opportunities. We are requiring them to foot the bill for our own lack of discipline and responsibility. Those who advocate budget cuts are often accused of lacking compassion. However, our failure to cut the budget betrays an astonishing lack of compassion for our children and grandchildren.

If we have any doubt where all of this is heading, we need only look across the Atlantic to the failing welfare states of Europe. Greece, for example, which has been living beyond its means for years, has been forced to adopt painful austerity measures as a condition to being bailed out by the rest of Europe. The announcement of these measures was greeted with widespread rioting. Clearly, the rioters believe that they are entitled to a welfare state that they can't afford, even if the taxpayers of other countries have to pay for it. This is a cautionary tale of how people, once they get used to welfare state benefits, develop a sense of entitlement that overwhelms their sense of reality, responsibility and fair play.

Greek Finance Minister Evangelos Venizelos addressed the rioting in a speech before Parliament: "We have to explain to all these indignant people who see their lives changing that what the country is experiencing is not the worst stage of the crisis," he said. "It is an anguished and necessary effort to avoid the ultimate, deepest and harshest level of the crisis. The difference between a difficult situation and a catastrophe is immense."[46]

America faces the same choice—the choice between a difficult situation and a catastrophe. Greece is a cautionary tale of what can happen to our government if we fail to make difficult choices before it's too late. But it's also a cautionary tale of what can happen to our spirit. Do we want to end up like the Greeks, raging against a reality of our own making, refusing to be held accountable for our own choices? Greece demonstrates how a welfare state results in the infantilization of a society, both in how it breeds dependence and how it breeds a sense of entitlement—with a child's lack of concern for how much things cost and who picks up the tab. These attitudes are inimical to the qualities of self-reliance and personal responsibility that have made America a great nation. My intention is not to attack the Greeks—they are a great and proud people who, like many of their fellow Europeans, have had their strength sapped by the seductive enslavement of the welfare state.

As hard as it may be for people on the left to admit, the Tea Party has been proven right. You can mock the funny hats, the misspelled (and sometimes offensive) signs and the yelling at town hall meetings, but the Tea Party has been absolutely right about its central issue: the federal debt is reaching crisis levels that will ruin us if we don't get it under control. Standard & Poor's acknowledged as much when it threatened to downgrade our credit rating if Congress didn't act to reduce the debt by $4 trillion—and by making good on that threat. [47] Thanks largely to the efforts of the Tea Party, it has become almost impossible for Democrats or Republicans to ignore the debt crisis.

This creates a new reality that liberals have no choice but to adapt to. The proud legacies of liberalism's most celebrated eras—the New Deal's Social Security program and the Great Society's Medicare—are heading for crisis and cannot survive in their current forms. The great new entitlement, Obamacare, faces an uncertain future—and it is hard to imagine how we can afford it. And in the fiscal climate that we're likely to face for the foreseeable future, further expansions of the welfare state are virtually out of the question.

At a time when their dreams and ambitions are colliding head-on with fiscal reality, liberals have to figure out what is really important to them. Here is how ConservaDave might attempt to walk Liberal Dave through the problem: "What you really want is a comprehensive social welfare state. That's not possible given the fiscal realities we face. So why don't you step back and ask yourself what you really wanted to accomplish by building that welfare state? Limited resources force us to prioritize, so what are the *most important* things you wanted to accomplish through the welfare state? Making sure that our entire society is as prosperous as it can be? Giving poor people the opportunity to lift themselves out of poverty? Making sure our children get a good education, and that poor, inner city children aren't disadvantaged throughout their lives because they attended dysfunctional schools? Ensuring that we all have access to good, affordable health care? Making sure we protect the environment?

"And recognize that in the real world, all of your objectives won't fit together seamlessly. You'll often have to choose between policies that further some of your objectives (protecting the environment, for example) but harm other of your objectives (creating economic opportunity, for example), but you work to find the proper balance. And once you prioritize what you want to achieve, be flexible and entertain new ideas about how to achieve it. You have a tendency to assume that it's government's job to fix every problem. Challenge your assumptions, and be open to other ways of achieving your objectives. Those other ways may be more cost-effective in some cases, and they may be more effective period."

ConservaDave has just outlined the case for a "Left-Hearted, Right-Minded" philosophy. We have entered an era where profligacy in the name of compassion is heartlessly uncompassionate to the young and those yet to be born. Liberals must find new ways to channel the compassion in their hearts—ways that can improve society today, without placing impossible burdens on those who would fight to improve it in the future. It is the thesis of this book that in this age of limited government resources, conservative policies are actually the best way to achieve the most essential liberal ideals. The chapters that follow will make that case for issue after issue. To kick that off, we'll be eavesdropping on a wide-ranging conversation between Liberal Dave and ConservaDave on capitalism, corporate greed, taxing the rich and much, much more.

5 LIBERAL DAVE VS. CONSERVADAVE: SOON TO BE A MAJOR MOTION PICTURE

There's an old Hollywood joke that everyone in Los Angeles has a script they're trying to get produced. I live in Los Angeles so, naturally, I have a script of my own.

My script is called *Liberal Dave vs. ConservaDave*, a title that's kind of reminiscent of the *Alien vs. Predator* movie that came out a few years back. But my script, unlike *Alien vs. Predator*, is not science fiction. It's more inspired by *My Dinner with Andre*, a 1981 film that consists entirely of two intellectuals having a conversation over dinner in a restaurant. My film will be just like *My Dinner with Andre*, except instead of two intellectuals we'll have Liberal Dave and ConservaDave; that substitution will require us to dumb down the conversation a great deal from the original. Oh, and because we're on a tight budget, we'll have to film in a much cheaper restaurant. I'm counting on no one remembering *My Dinner with Andre*, so that people will hail my work as bold and original.

I'm trying to get Brad Pitt to play both roles. Neither Liberal Dave nor ConservaDave looks anything like Brad Pitt, but America doesn't need to know that. Here, then, for the first time anywhere, is my original screenplay:

INTERIOR. PIZZARIA, DOWNTOWN MANHATTAN –
EVENING

CONSERVADAVE and LIBERAL DAVE are sharing a pizza. The
date is October 5, 2011, the day that Steve Jobs died and the 19th day
of the Occupy Wall Street protests in New York City.

> ### LIBERAL DAVE
> Well, thanks for inviting me out for pizza.

> ### CONSERVADAVE
> Thanks for coming. Always good to catch up
> with my Siamese Brain Twin.

> ### LIBERAL DAVE
> We can't go to McDonald's anymore since
> you went vegetarian. I'm glad you didn't go
> vegan; we can still go for pizza.

> ### CONSERVADAVE
> You're the one that's always preaching about
> compassion and the environment. How come
> *I'm* willing to sacrifice to have a cruelty-free,
> environmentally friendly diet and you're not?

> ### LIBERAL DAVE
> I need my protein.

> ### CONSERVADAVE
> Or maybe I just have the courage of your
> convictions.

LIBERAL DAVE

I'll ignore that. I'll just chalk it up to the sibling rivalry that inevitably arises when two people are competing for space in the same brain.

CONSERVADAVE

So, are you really going to join those Occupy Wall Street protests tomorrow?

LIBERAL DAVE

Yes, I really am. Wait.
(holds up his hand and pauses)
If you listen closely you can hear them from here.

CONSERVADAVE

I can smell them from here.

LIBERAL DAVE

Very funny. Anyway, wanna come with me?

CONSERVADAVE

Not really my style. I see those anti-Semitic protest signs on the web, those YouTube clips of people railing about "Jewish bankers"—a little too bigoted for my taste. Plus, from what I see, these people are extremely radical.

LIBERAL DAVE

That's completely not fair. You can't dismiss an entire movement as bigoted or extremist because of a few nutcases. Every movement

71

has some nutcases. You can't use that as an excuse to ignore some very legitimate points they're making.

CONSERVADAVE
Fair enough. Now can we apply that same rule to the Tea Party?

LIBERAL DAVE
Consistency is the hobgoblin of small minds.

CONSERVADAVE
That's a good motto for you. It'll help you win arguments that you'd otherwise lose.

LIBERAL DAVE
Whatever. But hey, maybe this is like our Tea Party.

CONSERVADAVE
Except Tea Party demonstrators never do anything that'll get 'em arrested, they clean up their mess, they don't try to disrupt the lives of their communities to make their point, they proudly wave the American flag, they don't demand that their fellow taxpayers give them free stuff—

LIBERAL DAVE
Right, right, right. I get it. The Tea Baggers are perfect.

CONSERVADAVE

OK but tell me for real why you want to go
down there.

LIBERAL DAVE

I just feel that I was meant to be down there.
Those kids are so idealistic down there. I was
just a kid when they had all those protests
against the Viet Nam War. I was too young to
join them, but I wanted to. Even as a kid I got
caught up in the spirit of what they were
doing. Against all odds, they took to the
streets and changed the world. Maybe those
kids down in Zuccotti Park are going to
change the world again. I wanna be a part of
it this time.

CONSERVADAVE

Sounds like you're mostly just caught up in
the romance of being part of a protest
movement.

LIBERAL DAVE

That's not fair.

CONSERVADAVE

I just get the feeling that those protestors feel
like they're being noble, like they're speaking
truth to power and all that. But it's not
enough to feel noble, to feel good about
yourself. It's not enough to have good
intentions. You have to do your homework,
and really think through all of the unintended
consequences of what you're advocating.

Because vulnerable people would be hurt if
we actually did what you guys want us to do.
In my humble opinion, the policies you guys
support would destroy the entire economy and
poor people would be hurt the most. And in
my humble opinion, you should be protesting
against the federal government and not against
Wall Street.

LIBERAL DAVE

Well, on behalf of the entire movement, thank
you for your humble opinions. But I don't
think you have a good idea of what we're
fighting for.

CONSERVADAVE

OK, so educate me. How exactly do you want
to change the world?

LIBERAL DAVE

Well, for starters, I wanna see the rich pay
their fair share of taxes.

CONSERVADAVE

So what would be their fair share? The richest
one percent contributes about 40 percent of
our income tax revenues. The top 10 percent
pays about 70 percent. The bottom 50 percent
pays less than three percent.[48] About 47
percent pay no income tax at all.[49] Am I
missing something?

LIBERAL DAVE

Yes, you are. You're just talking about
federal income tax. The poor pay other taxes.

CONSERVADAVE

Yeah, and the rich pay those other taxes as
well. Again, am I missing something?

LIBERAL DAVE

Maybe *I'm* missing something. I'm missing
why you have so much sympathy for rich
people and so little sympathy for poor people.

CONSERVADAVE

Wrong on both counts, Kemo Sabe. I don't
have sympathy for rich people. And I do care
about poor people. I used to be one.

LIBERAL DAVE

Yeah, me too. If you really do care about
poor people, that's pretty unusual for a
conservative.

CONSERVADAVE

Not fair and not true. Conservatives give a lot
more to charity than liberals do.

LIBERAL DAVE

That's because conservatives are richer than
liberals.

CONSERVADAVE

Wrong again, Buzzard Breath. Liberals are
richer than conservatives—on average, at

75

least—but conservatives still give 30 percent more to charity.[50] I don't give liberals credit for being compassionate just because they vote to give other people's money to programs that they *say* will help the poor—and then they don't even care about whether those programs work or not.

LIBERAL DAVE

Well that's a pretty harsh generalization. Buzzard Breath? From my own freaking alter ego no less.

CONSERVADAVE

That's from the old Johnny Carson shows I watch on Hulu. You don't really have buzzard breath.

LIBERAL DAVE

OK, so you care about poor people. Congratulations. But if you don't have sympathy for rich people, as you claim, how come you don't want to raise their taxes?

CONSERVADAVE

I don't want to raise *anybody's* taxes in a bad economy.

LIBERAL DAVE

Well poor people can't afford to pay more. Rich people can.

CONSERVADAVE

I agree with you. Rich people can afford to
pay more. If you increase their taxes, they'll
still be rich. They'll still have their big
homes, their fancy cars, their jet-setting
lifestyles. Will I shed a tear for some rich guy
who has to tighten his belt because of a tax
hike, and put off buying that second corporate
jet? No, I will not. But you're missing the
point.

LIBERAL DAVE

So what *is* the point?

CONSERVADAVE

I'm not worried about hurting the rich. I'm
worried about hurting the rest of us.

LIBERAL DAVE

How would raising taxes on the rich hurt the
rest of us? Would we all start feeling
emotionally depressed out of empathy for the
rich because they have to pay more taxes?

CONSERVADAVE

No, but we might start feeling economically
depressed if the rich invest less in our
economy. Like it or not, the rich are the ones
with the greatest ability and the greatest
inclination to invest in our economy. How do
you think businesses get the money they need
to get started, to expand, to hire people? From
investors. We need rich people to invest—in
other people's businesses or their own

businesses—to create jobs. Investment creates economic activity that reverberates through the whole economy. Businesses and workers have more money to spend and invest, which helps other businesses and other workers, and so on and so on, all of which creates income that the government can tax for the revenues it needs to do its thing. Raising taxes on the rich will mean that they'll have less money to invest. It'll also mean that they'll have less incentive to invest the money they have, because they'll get to keep less of the profits. The result will be fewer jobs, which is absolutely the worst possible thing for the people who are struggling the most.

LIBERAL DAVE

Do you really mean to tell me that raising taxes on the rich a few percentage points is going to have an impact on jobs?

CONSERVADAVE

For an individual rich guy, the tax increase may or may not be overly dramatic. But if we're talking about raising hundreds of billions of dollars by taxing the rich, that's hundreds of billions of dollars that won't be available for them to invest. That could mean that a lot of jobs that would have been created won't be.

LIBERAL DAVE

Yeah, but the government can create jobs by investing the money it taxes from rich people.

CONSERVADAVE

Except that government is much less efficient
and effective in creating jobs. Bureaucrats
don't do as good a job at picking good
investments as private investors, because
bureaucrats don't have their own money at
stake. And if they were good at making
business decisions, they'd be in business.
That's why they flush billions of dollars down
the toilet with "investments" like Solyndra.
Why should we suck money out of the hands
of people who would do a better job of putting
it to productive use? Do you really think
government would do a better job of putting
that money to productive use? What did
Obama's stimulus bill get us other than
hundreds of billions of dollars deeper in debt?

LIBERAL DAVE

Paul Krugman says that the stimulus failed
because it was too small. And he won a
Nobel Prize in economics. Where's *your*
Nobel Prize, buddy?

CONSERVADAVE

I'm still working on it. But I just had a séance
last night with two other Nobel Prize-winning
economists, Milton Friedman and Friedrich
Hayek, and they both personally told me that
Krugman is full of crap. So there you have it,
two against one.

LIBERAL DAVE
Well that certainly settles *that*!

CONSERVADAVE
And speaking of dead economists, liberals like
to invoke the ghost of John Maynard Keynes
to justify huge amounts of government
spending to fight a recession. But here's how
I see it: Government can only create jobs by
taxing wealth created by the private sector.
The more you try to create jobs by expanding
government, the more you overburden the
very private sector that you need to pay for all
this government extravagance. That's like a
Ponzi Scheme that you can only sustain for so
long, as we're seeing in Europe.
Experimenting with Keynesianism might not
have been as dangerous when our debt burden
was manageable. But we have a massive debt
burden now. Hundreds of billions of dollars
are being sucked out of our economy just to
pay interest on our debt. If we keep adding to
our debt with these grand government job-
creation schemes, we might crush our
economy under the weight of the government.

LIBERAL DAVE
So says the amateur armchair economist who
has not won a Nobel Prize.

CONSERVADAVE
Well John Maynard Keynes and I are actually
of equal stature, because we both haven't won
the Nobel Prize for economics. But I forgot to

mention that I *was* recently awarded the Nobel Prize for Common Sense. I just don't like to brag about it.

LIBERAL DAVE

Humble as always. But if raising taxes on the rich would hurt job creation, why was our economy so strong under Clinton when tax rates were higher?

CONSERVADAVE

There were other things going on in during the Clinton years that made our economy strong. We had a dot.com boom—turned out to be a bubble, but we didn't know that until after he left office. When you have positive things going on in the economy, it can overcome the negative effect that tax increases have on job creation. When the economy isn't growing on its own steam, though, it's crazy to raise taxes. Then you're just killing jobs at a time when you desperately need to create jobs. Even Bill Clinton said you shouldn't raise taxes in a down economy.[51] For goodness sake, even Barack Obama used to say that.[52]

LIBERAL DAVE

Yeah, but what about fairness? Why shouldn't the rich pay more when people are struggling?

CONSERVADAVE

My point is that making the rich pay more will make the struggle worse, not better, for the guy who desperately needs a job. Let's get real for a minute. Let's say you're unemployed. Which would you rather have: a job, or the satisfaction of knowing that those rich bastards are paying more taxes? If I offered you a job that you really wanted and needed, would you really give a flying bleep about how much some rich guy you'll never meet is paying in taxes?

LIBERAL DAVE

Of course I'd rather have the job, but I still think it's un-American for the rich not to pay their fair share in taxes.

CONSERVADAVE

Well, if the richest one percent is paying 40 percent of the taxes, I'd say they *are* paying their fair share. But what's really un-American is getting upset that rich people are getting rich instead of figuring out how to make *yourself* rich. We're not Europeans. The American Way is to look at successful people as a source of inspiration, not envy. We were both able to make something of ourselves in spite of where we came from. That's the American Dream. If you stop letting rich people be rich, then poor people won't be able to get rich either. That's called socialism: everybody's equally poor—except for the ruling elite, of course. Socialism doesn't work because it runs counter to human nature. And it's very un-American. I mean honestly, what real American would say, "I'd rather stay poor if it would keep some other guy who I don't know from getting richer"? What kind of misguided sense of fairness is that?

LIBERAL DAVE

What misguided sense of fairness allows certain businesses to get special tax breaks just because they can afford to hire good lobbyists?

CONSERVADAVE

I agree with you on that. We should get rid of those special tax breaks. They distort the free market. But if we get rid of those tax breaks we also have to lower tax rates, or else we're just sucking money out of the private economy. We need a fairer and flatter system that gets rid of loopholes, lowers rates and encourages economic growth.

LIBERAL DAVE

We might be able to agree on that. Let's change the subject. It's more fun to argue.

CONSERVADAVE

Well if you're still set on going down to Occupy Wall Street, we have plenty left to argue about. The protestors down there want to expand the government and I want to shrink it.

LIBERAL DAVE
Why do you conservatives hate government so much? We're a democracy. The government is *us*.

CONSERVADAVE
Well thanks for conceding that we're a democracy. Your comrades have been calling Zuccotti Park our Tahrir Square, and saying we need our own Arab Spring. I was beginning to think that we were living in a fascist dictatorship, and those brave protestors were risking their lives to bring us democracy.

LIBERAL DAVE
They may not be risking their lives, but they're definitely fighting to make our democracy more responsive to the needs of the people.

CONSERVADAVE
Then they should be fighting for limited government. Look, you say that government is us. Well government starts out as us, but then "us" gets put through a process and gets distorted until something very different comes out the other end. Saying "government is us" is sort of like saying that the excrement we're going to produce tomorrow is the pizza we're eating now.

LIBERAL DAVE

Your analogy stinks, if I may say so. And
when did you start hating government so
much? Did you join a militia or something?

CONSERVADAVE

No, no, I don't hate government. Maybe
excrement's a little too strong. But here's the
thing about government. It's made up of two
kinds of people. First you have the
Bureaucrats—the career civil servants. Some
of them are really smart and capable, but some
of them are worthless and it's almost
impossible to fire them. But even the smartest
Bureaucrats can't possibly be smart enough to
micromanage an economy. That's why the
Soviet Union collapsed. The Bureaucrats are
overseen by the Politicos. These are the ones
who come and go with whatever
administration gets elected. Like the
Bureaucrats, some of the Politicos are smart
and capable—but many of them are highly
partisan and are mostly focused on rewarding
their friends and punishing their enemies.
Both the Politicos and the Bureaucrats are
obsessed with keeping their own jobs. That's
why Politicos put a positive spin on
everything their administration does, no
matter how lousy. And hell hath no fury like
a Bureaucrat who's been told that his job may
no longer be necessary. So I kind of jumble
the Politicos and the Bureaucrats together and
call them all Politicrats. If I ever need a
reminder that government is not the solution

to every problem, I just think about all of the
Politicrats running the government.

LIBERAL DAVE

Well once again, you're wrong about what the
protestors are fighting for. They don't like the
Politicrats any more than you do. There's
something very special going on here that
you're not attuned to. This is the start of a
Worldwide Wiki Revolution where people are
going to take back the power from the special
interests—and yes, from the Politicrats as
well.

CONSERVADAVE

Worldwide Wiki Revolution? "Wiki"?

LIBERAL DAVE

Yeah, Wiki. It's Hawaiian for "quick." You
should know that, Dude, you're Polynesian.

CONSERVADAVE

Yeah, like the Wiki Wiki Shuttle in Honolulu.

LIBERAL DAVE

Funny you should say that. Wiki is actually
software that allows people from anywhere to
collaborate with one another, and it really *was*
named after the Wiki Wiki Shuttle. But the
"Wiki" concept has grown way beyond the
software. It's come to mean a continuous,
real-time, ongoing collaboration among
millions of people around the world who don't
even know each other. That's how these

protests are springing up everywhere. That's how strangers from all over the world have built Wikipedia into something that people find more useful than encyclopedias written by professional experts. Wiki is all about direct, real-time democracy and empowerment. It's a brand new model for building communities and society.

                    CONSERVADAVE
I don't think it's new at all. It sounds like capitalism to me.

                    LIBERAL DAVE
Oh, bite your tongue.

                    CONSERVADAVE
I'm serious. A free market economy is the greatest Wiki collaboration of all. Every day, millions of people who don't know each other send billions of signals about what they want and need—and how much they're willing to pay to satisfy each of their wants and needs. And the businesses that do the best job of providing people with what they want and need are rewarded the most. Businesses respond to these signals sent out by the people by directing resources to the uses that are likely to provide the highest reward. So capitalism causes resources to be allocated in a way that is most responsive to what people want and need. How's that for direct, real-time democracy and empowerment? It's all

based on what the people want and need.
Power to the people!

LIBERAL DAVE
Where's the flag? I need to salute something
right away!

CONSERVADAVE
And how do we set prices under capitalism?
Do we let the Politicrats do it? No! We
crowd-source it to the Wiki wisdom of the
masses. And do we let the Politicrats decide
how much everyone gets paid? No! The
Politicrats are no match for the Wiki Wisdom
of the Market. The Wiki Wisdom processes
billions of signals, billions of data points, in a
way that even the most brilliant Politicrat
could never hope to replicate.

LIBERAL DAVE
Yeah, well your brilliant capitalism resulted in
a bunch of failed companies getting bailed out
by the Politicrats, and then their greedy
bastard CEOs still got paid obscene amounts
of money.

CONSERVADAVE
You've got that wrong, my friend. The
Politicrats are the ones that caused the mess.
That's what happens when Politicrats interfere
with the direct, real-time democracy of the
Wiki Wisdom of the Market.

LIBERAL DAVE

But don't the Politicrats represent our
democracy? Are you saying that our
democracy is interfering with democracy?

CONSERVADAVE

We're talking about two different types of
democracy. The free market is the direct,
real-time democracy that you waxed eloquent
about in your moving homage to Wikipedia.
It is the truest, purest expression of people's
wants and needs. The Politicrats represent a
more plodding, politicized version of
democracy. The ability to fire leaders once
every four years does not provide the real-
time responsiveness that the continuously
updated Wiki Wisdom of the Market provides.
And when the Politicrats try to overrule the
Wiki Wisdom of the Market, you always get
unintended consequences. It's like when a fat
person puts on a girdle. You try to squeeze
things into control in one area but something
pops out somewhere else.

LIBERAL DAVE

A little mean-spirited conservative humor
there.

CONSERVADAVE

But to give you an example: You brought up
the bailouts. First of all, government bailouts
are not capitalism. They're Politicrat
interference with the Wiki Wisdom of the
Market. Sometimes the Wiki Wisdom says

that businesses that made bad choices need to fail, and their assets and employees need to be picked up by businesses that can do a better job of responding to the market signals put out by the people.

LIBERAL DAVE

Government bailouts *are* capitalism—*crony* capitalism. The businesses with the best lobbyists, who make the most donations, who have the most influence, are the ones who'll get bailed out when they mess up. That's what my comrades, as you call them, are protesting down in Zuccotti Square.

CONSERVADAVE

And they're right to be protesting that. But crony capitalism isn't capitalism. It's corruption. It's Politicrats—particularly the Politicos—overruling the Wiki Wisdom of the Market to benefit their donors and other pals.

LIBERAL DAVE

So obviously we should ban corporations from contributing to politicians.

CONSERVADAVE

And let unions keep contributing? I don't think so. Those public sector unions have a great racket going on. They give tons of money to politicians—politicians of your ilk. Those politicians turn around and pass laws requiring public sector workers to join the union and pay dues, whether they want to or not. And then a good chunk of those dues goes right back into the campaign coffers of those politicians to keep them in office. And the politicians say thank you by approving super-generous contracts that are breaking the backs of the taxpayers.

LIBERAL DAVE

OK, so your answer is to do nothing?

CONSERVADAVE

My answer is to reduce the role of government in our lives. I mean think about it. What if government didn't control as much? What if we drastically cut back the contracts government got to award, the grants, loans and loan guarantees government got to hand out, the number of decisions it got to make that affected the economy? If government didn't impose itself so much on our economy, then businesses, unions and other special interests wouldn't feel as compelled to flood politicians with cash and swarm them with lobbyists to try to rig the system in their favor.

LIBERAL DAVE

But that's exactly what the Occupy Wall Street folks want to stop.

CONSERVADAVE

Yeah, but they're missing the point. Your comrades say they're against crony capitalism, but then they want to expand the role of government like we've never seen before.

And then we'll end up with something that's
much worse even than crony capitalism—
crony socialism. Limited government is the
best antidote to crony capitalism. The more
power you concentrate in government, the
more government becomes the target for
manipulation by powerful, influential interests
who are looking out for themselves and
couldn't care less what the people want.

LIBERAL DAVE
What if we had a benevolent socialist
dictatorship?

CONSERVADAVE
What if we had unicorns to sing us lullabies at
night? And what self-respecting American
would rather live under a dictatorship than be
free? Even socialists want to be free—they
just want to control everybody else.

LIBERAL DAVE
But at least under socialism, you wouldn't
have the big, powerful, private corporations to
manipulate the government.

CONSERVADAVE
Don't kid yourself. Every single society has
powerful, influential interests that are intent
on manipulating the system—the ruling party,
the state-owned corporations, the military, the
old families, or whatever. Socialist and
communist dictatorships all preach
egalitarianism, but each and every one of them

has had a ruling elite that lived much better than everyone else. The more you concentrate power, the easier it is for the ruling elite to control things and the harder it is for everybody else to prosper. A true free market democracy with limited government is the closest thing to the Wiki ethic. The more you move towards socialism and larger government, the more anti-Wiki you become.

LIBERAL DAVE

I just taught you that freaking word and you already think you're a Wiki expert.

CONSERVADAVE

I love the concept. I'm all about the Wiki now.

LIBERAL DAVE

You're all about the capitalism, which completely failed us in '08.

CONSERVADAVE

Wrong again, Pizza Breath. The financial crisis was a failure of government, not of capitalism. If we had just allowed the banks to follow the Wiki Wisdom of the Market, they would never have made all those risky mortgage loans that got us into that mess. But the Politicrats bullied the banks into making loans they shouldn't have made—all for a laudable goal, of course: to allow more people to own homes. And the Politicrats at Fannie Mae and Freddie Mac created a huge market for those risky loans, raising huge sums of money from investors and using that money to buy millions of risky loans from their original lenders. This ensured that the lenders would have a continuous supply of money to make new risky loans. Wall Street joined the effort, bringing in additional investor money to support home loans for people with lower incomes. And by the time the house of cards came tumbling down, the market that the Politicrats had created was so big that its collapse led the entire world into a financial and economic crisis. Millions and millions of people around the world have been hurt by all of this. And do you know what the irony is?

LIBERAL DAVE
Of course not. I need you to tell it to me.

CONSERVADAVE
The irony is that this was caused by well-meaning policies where the Politicrats tried to overrule the Wiki Wisdom of the Market in order to help people. They wanted to help lower income people own homes, which is a noble goal. But as a result of what they did, billions of people from all over the world have been hurt. People have lost their jobs, lost their homes, and seen the value of everything they've worked so hard for in their lives go down the drain. And the people who have been hurt the most by this economic disaster have been the poor, the very people that the

Politicrats thought they were helping. That's the kind of thing that made me turn away from liberalism. It's not enough to have good intentions. In the real world, where real people's lives and livelihoods are at stake, results matter. Consequences matter.

LIBERAL DAVE
How come no one went to jail?

CONSERVADAVE
Who should we have sent to jail? Barney Frank and the Democrats, for thwarting Republican efforts to reign in Fannie and Freddie when there was still a chance to avert the crisis?

LIBERAL DAVE
I was talking about the lenders and the people on Wall Street.

CONSERVADAVE
You want to send them to jail? For what? For succumbing to the pressure that the Politicrats were putting on them to make these bad loans? For doing what the Politicrats wanted them to do—raising funds to support loans for the poor? They didn't break the law, unless stuff went on that we don't know about. They just responded to incentives that were artificially created by government. They did what any businesspeople put in their position would do, trying to succeed under the rules and incentives set up by the government.

They did what the Politicrats wanted them to do, contrary to the Wiki Wisdom of the Market.

LIBERAL DAVE
(looking down at his iPhone)
Hey, I don't want to interrupt your fascinating filibuster here, but Steve Jobs died.

CONSERVADAVE
What? Are you serious? That's so sad. He was a hero of mine.

LIBERAL DAVE
He was a hero of mine, too.

CONSERVADAVE
A hero of yours? Weren't you just talking about greedy bastard CEOs who make obscene amounts of money? Apple's the richest company in America, and Steve Jobs was a multi-gazillionaire. Doesn't that make him the type of monster that you and your comrades would have wanted to guillotine?

LIBERAL DAVE
Oh, give me a freaking break. He was a great visionary. I love my iPhone. And if I could afford an iPad, I would love that too.

CONSERVADAVE
So why do you worship Steve Jobs, who's one of the richest guys of all, and you want to put the Wall Street bankers in jail?

LIBERAL DAVE
Steve Jobs earned every penny. He created
things. He brought us products that made our
lives better. Those vultures on Wall Street
just move money around and exploit people.

CONSERVADAVE
How do you think people like Steve Jobs are
able to bring us all those wonderful products
that make our lives better? Those "vultures"
who "just move money around" are the ones
that enable those visionary entrepreneurs raise
the funds to develop their products. And
you're right, a lot of those products do make
our lives better—and not just fun things like
iPods. Think of all the medical devices and
drugs that save people's lives, the software
that helps poor kids learn, the agricultural
innovations that help people in the Third
World feed themselves—the list goes on and
on. Millions of important inventions would
never see the light of day if we didn't have
super-smart investment bankers who work
100 hours a week raising money for
entrepreneurs, if we didn't have commercial
bankers working with them to provide loans,
if we didn't have investors willing to risk their
money. If some of these people get rewarded
handsomely for their special skills, energy and
daring, so be it. A lot of middle class jobs
depend on these folks, both in the financial
services industry and in the multitude of
industries they raise money for. And do you

think New York could afford its generous welfare state without the wealth generated by these folks?

LIBERAL DAVE

Good for them. But some of them still make too damn much money.

CONSERVADAVE

What about LeBron James. Does he make too damn much money?

LIBERAL DAVE

Of course he does. I hate the Miami Heat.

CONSERVADAVE

OK, then what about Kobe Bryant?

LIBERAL DAVE

That's a different story.

CONSERVADAVE

What about all those filthy rich celebrities that support Occupy Wall Street—Michael Moore, Tim Robbins, Kanye West, Alec Baldwin, Russell Simmons, Russell Brand, Katy Perry—do they make too damn much money?

LIBERAL DAVE

I don't think so. They're all very talented people. They bring joy to the world through their entertainment. And they don't exploit anyone.

CONSERVADAVE

By "exploit" people, do you mean *employ* people? Is your rule that rich people are OK as long as they're athletes or entertainers, but rich people who actually create jobs for others are bad?

LIBERAL DAVE

My rule is that some people make too damn much money. Not all rich people, but definitely some.

CONSERVADAVE

And who gets to get to decide who's making too damn much money? Do you want the Politicrats to make that decision, or should we leave it to the Wiki Wisdom of the Market?

LIBERAL DAVE

Well, I can guess how you want me to answer that question.

CONSERVADAVE

Damn right. If we let the Politicrats control who can make what, the Politicrats will make damn sure their supporters are overpaid and their opponents are underpaid.

LIBERAL DAVE

Well the Wiki Wisdom of the Market doesn't always work so well. What about when some CEO makes millions of dollars even as he drives his company into the ground?

CONSERVADAVE
And what about when one of those movie
stars visiting Occupy Wall Street gets paid
millions of dollars for a movie that bombs?
No system is perfect, but the Wiki Wisdom of
the Market corrects itself a lot quicker and a
lot better than the plodding, highly politicized
bureaucracy of government.

LIBERAL DAVE
Well average workers don't get to negotiate
multi-million dollar deals for themselves.
Don't you care about income inequality?

CONSERVADAVE
You can't get rid of income inequality without
destroying the incentives that lead to
productivity—the productivity that allows
capitalism to lift so many people out of
poverty. I'm OK with income inequality as
long as people who start at the bottom like we
did have a chance to work their way up.
That's why we have to fix our educational
system, which is the subject of another pizza.

LIBERAL DAVE
So what you're saying is that accepting
poverty is the price we have to pay to enjoy
the wonders of the Wiki Wisdom of the
Market. And if I hear that phrase one more
time I think I'm going to regurgitate my pizza.

CONSERVADAVE

That's not what I'm saying. You're confusing
income inequality with poverty. Capitalism
has lifted more people out of poverty than any
other economic system in history.[53]
Capitalism provides better for the poor than
any other system, and has allowed billions to
no longer be poor.[54] It's the best anti-poverty
program ever invented. C'mon, tell me you
agree with me now because I'm getting tired
of talking.

LIBERAL DAVE

You never get tired of talking.

CONSERVADAVE

Hey, and do me a favor when you get down to
Zuccotti Square. Tell your comrades that the
things they're advocating would have a
disastrous effect on the poor. Then ask them:
Why do you hate poor people so much?

LIBERAL DAVE

I'll be sure to ask them that.

CONSERVADAVE

Oh and one more thing. Get me one of those
"Occupy Wall Street" T-shirts.

LIBERAL DAVE

You can order one yourself online. They
accept Visa and Mastercard.

CONSERVADAVE
Good deal. So, have I gotten through to you?
Are you still a liberal?

LIBERAL DAVE
I'll always be a liberal. That's why they call
me Liberal Dave. As they used to say in the
Old West, this brain isn't big enough for the
two of us.

CONSERVADAVE
Your brain isn't big enough, period.

LIBERAL DAVE
Be that as it may. Anything else you want to
get off your chest?

CONSERVADAVE
Yeah. Mom always liked you best.

LIBERAL DAVE
Of course she did. She was in the union.

Fade to black. Roll credits.

Postscript: I was walking down the street recently and ran into a
friend of mine. "Hey Dave," he smiled. "I think you've been
working too hard. I saw you coming from a block away, and you
were muttering to yourself like some crazy person." If only you
knew, I thought. I wasn't talking to myself. Liberal Dave was
talking to ConservaDave.

6 EDUCATION: "THE GREAT CIVIL RIGHTS ISSUE OF OUR TIME"

Liberal Dave's mom was a schoolteacher. So was ConservaDave's for that matter. She taught third grade at Anne Beers Elementary School, an inner city school that was just a few miles down Alabama Avenue from the family's apartment in Southeast D.C.

Liberal Dave's mom knew the D.C. public school system as well as anyone. Not only did she teach in the system, but she attended D.C. public schools from the time the family moved down from the Bronx when she was small until she graduated from Anacostia High School. Her familiarity with D.C. public schools made her absolutely certain of one thing: come hell or high water, there was no way that Liberal Dave was going to attend them. Liberal Dave would not have gone to Anne Beers; that was the next school over. But Liberal Dave's mom was well familiar with the school that her son would have attended, Stanton Elementary. It was the same school that Liberal Dave's mom and Uncle Bill had attended. Come hell or high water, there was no way....

Fortunately for Liberal Dave, his family was able to pool their resources to send him to Jewish parochial school in Northwest D.C.—"yeshiva," as they call it. The environment couldn't have been more different than what he would have experienced at Stanton. And Liberal Dave got a solid educational foundation in parochial school. More importantly, he was placed in an environment where the peer pressure was to achieve academically, where teachers had high expectations of students, and students had high expectations of themselves. These expectations became self-fulfilling, and Liberal Dave found himself on a trajectory where high school led naturally to college (and a scholarship), college led naturally to professional school, and professional school led naturally to a good career. Of course, it wasn't quite as easy as that—it never is. But there is no doubt that Liberal Dave's path in life would have been much more difficult had it not been for the expectations that were instilled in him back in elementary school.

Liberal Dave's mother was following a long-standing tradition in the Nation's Capital: anyone who had the choice to avoid D.C. public schools did so—even if the "choice" required putting the family through financial hardship. Those for whom financial hardship was not an issue, including the powerful national politicians who lived in Washington, would never have dreamed of sending their children to D.C. public schools.

One notable exception, of course, was Amy Carter, who was still in elementary school when her father was elected President in 1976. President Jimmy Carter made a point of enrolling Amy in Thaddeus Stevens Elementary School, a predominantly African-American public school five blocks from the White House. Amy thus became the only child of a sitting president to attend public school since little Quentin Roosevelt (son of Theodore) did so in 1906.[55]

The Carters' decision to enroll their daughter at Stevens is worthy of both praise and criticism—praise because it was a powerful morale boost to a struggling and much-maligned school system; criticism because the President appeared to also be boosting his own image as a "regular guy" at the expense of his own daughter's welfare. Amy reportedly had a hard time making friends at Stevens, and wasn't allowed to play outside at recess because of security concerns.[56] And even assuming that she got a good education in public school, would she not have been served much better by one of the internationally renowned private schools that her parents could have sent her to? Ironically, the Carters' symbolic move was a double-edged sword for D.C.'s public schools: the publicity generated by the First Family's "vote of confidence" brought national attention to why the D.C. public school system had been so disparaged in the first place.

When the Clintons came to town after the 1992 elections, questions inevitably arose as to whether their young daughter Chelsea would follow in Amy's footsteps. *The New York Times* reported that the Clintons did "not want their 12-year-old daughter to suffer for the sake of making a political statement."[57] Could that have been a swipe at President Carter? In any event, Chelsea Clinton was sent to Sidwell Friends School, the same exclusive private academy that Sasha and Malia Obama enrolled in 16 years later.

Of course, most children in Washington don't have the option of escaping their failing neighborhood schools. The heartbreaking documentary *Waiting for Superman* tells the story of five children from around the country whose parents are trying desperately to get them into charter schools.

Charter schools, which are authorized in most states, are public schools that operate in many ways like private schools: they are not subject to the rules and regulations of traditional public schools. Most of them are not unionized. But unlike private schools, they cannot charge tuition; they are funded by public money and, in some cases, private donations. The schools are called "charter schools" because each has a charter which spells out performance standards that it is expected to meet. Depending on the state, charters can be issued by local school districts, an independent authority, or the state itself. Like private schools, attendance at charter schools is voluntary. Students aren't limited to charter schools in their neighborhood; they can attend one across town.

The idea of charter schools, which were first authorized in the U.S. by a 1991 Minnesota law and have since spread quickly around the country, is that schools might perform better if they're freed from stifling bureaucracy. There is also the notion that one size doesn't fit all, and many charter schools specialize in particular areas (math and science, for example).

The best performing charter schools are oversubscribed, and must choose students based on a lottery. That provides the drama in *Waiting for Superman*, which culminates with each of the five students waiting anxiously to see if their number is called. The film's climax is absolutely nerve-wracking, because we have come to know each of the students over the course of the film and realize how much is at stake.

Each of the film's young stars has a compelling story:[58]

Anthony is an African-American fifth-grader from Liberal Dave's old hometown, Washington, D.C. He never knew his mother; his father, a drug addict, died in 2004. He now lives with his grandparents in a poor, high-crime neighborhood. His grandparents are desperate to get him into SEED Charter School, a boarding school which sends 90 percent of its students on to college. Getting into SEED would enable Anthony to escape his dangerous neighborhood and the failing middle school that he is slated to attend.

Daisy, also a fifth-grader, lives across the country in the poor Mexican-American neighborhood of East Los Angeles. She wants to be a doctor, has chosen the college that she wants to attend and has already written to that college to request admission. Only 40 percent of the students in her neighborhood graduate high school. Neither of her parents graduated high school—her mother works as a janitor and her father is currently unemployed. Daisy lives near one of the best charter schools in Los Angeles, KIPP LA PREP; it is the kind of school that can prepare her for her dream of becoming a doctor. The traditional public schools in her neighborhood, on the other hand, are among the worst in the city. Daisy wants more than anything to get into KIPP, but the odds are against her. The school is greatly oversubscribed, with 135 applicants competing for only 10 slots. Daisy only has a 14 percent chance of winning the lottery.

First-grader Francisco is being raised by his single mother in the Bronx. His mother, Maria, is determined to get Francisco out of the public school in their inner city neighborhood so he can get a proper education. She had applied for Francisco to attend seven charter schools, but was rejected each time. She now sees Harlem Success Academy, an excellent charter school that would be a 45-minute commute from their home, as Francisco's last chance. Francisco will be one of 792 applicants vying for 40 slots at Harlem Success Academy; he has a five percent chance of success.

Competing to get into the same school is Bianca, an African-American kindergartener who lives across the river from Francisco in Harlem. Bianca is also being raised by a single mother, Nakia, who has been paying $500 per month to send her daughter to a Catholic school but can no longer afford it. Nakia never attended college but is determined that Bianca will. The two are pinning their hopes on Bianca's five percent chance of winning one of the prized slots at Harlem Success Academy.

Which, if any, of our young protagonists will win the lottery? I'm not going to spoil the suspense, because I want everyone who hasn't already done so to see the movie. But the premise should have any right-thinking American—and left-thinking Americans as well—furious. Why in the world should any American child's opportunity for a decent education—and hence a decent future—depend on winning a lottery against almost impossible odds? Why are inner city parents so desperate for their children to "escape" their neighborhood public schools, as if they were prisons? Public schools are supposed to be the great equalizer in our society, empowering poor kids with free education to overcome the disadvantages of their birth; instead they've become the great stratifier, freezing those disadvantages into place. Public schools have become an obstacle to the class mobility that they are intended to facilitate.

President George W. Bush called education the "great civil rights issue of our time." Years later, President Barack Obama said it as well. In becoming the first person of color to be elected President, Barack Obama has lent some validation to the famous American notion that every child can grow up to be President of the United States. That notion was clearly a myth for much of our history, particularly when slavery and Jim Crow prevailed in the South. But it sure felt like less of a myth the night Barack Obama was elected.

Obama graduated from Punahou School, an exclusive private prep school in Hawaii. The color of his skin did not prevent him from growing up to be President. But could he ever have made it that far had he been stuck in one of those dysfunctional public schools that Anthony, Daisy, Francisco and Bianca were trying to escape? For these children and millions like them, failing public schools are an infinitely greater obstacle to their ability to succeed in life than the color of their skin. Education is indeed the great civil rights issue of our time.

America's educational problems aren't confined to the inner city. U.S. 15-year-olds rank 25th out of 34 developed countries in mathematics literacy, 17th in science literacy and only slightly better—14th—in reading literacy.[59] But take heart, proud Americans, because there is one category where we rank first: spending per pupil.[60]

Clearly we're getting lousy value for our generous spending on education. There is perhaps no more pathetic example than Liberal Dave's old hometown. A 2007 *Washington Post* article illustrated why Liberal Dave's mom was so adamant about keeping her son out of the D.C. public school system—and why Anthony's grandparents were praying so hard that he would win the SEED Charter School lottery. The *Post* reported that D.C. spent just under $13,000 per pupil each year, ranking third among the 100 largest school districts in the nation. But in both reading and math, D.C. came in last out of 11 major city school districts. Not surprisingly, the poor were particularly ill-served: In the nation as a whole, 33 percent of poor fourth-graders lacked basic math skills, but that figure was almost twice as high—62 percent—for poor fourth-graders in D.C. The results were even worse for poor eighth-graders in D.C.: 74 percent of them lacked basic math skills, compared to 49 percent of poor eighth-graders nationally.

But D.C. did manage to take first place in one category: the percentage of its education budget spent on administration. The other side of that coin, of course, is that D.C. ranked dead last out of the 100 largest school districts in percentage of budget spent on teachers and instruction. Most D.C. education dollars get siphoned off for administration and who-knows-what, never making it to the classroom.[61]

Waiting for Superman provides additional insights on why we get such a poor return on our investment in elementary and secondary education. At the risk of grossly oversimplifying the wealth of information and analysis presented in *Superman*, here is how I would characterize the film's central argument: Great teachers are the key to a great educational system. As successful charter schools have shown, even students from the most disadvantaged backgrounds can thrive in classrooms run by great teachers. We therefore need to reward the great teachers that we have so we can keep them, and attract new great teachers to replace the bad ones. We can't do this, however, if we refuse to get rid of the bad teachers. If we keep paying teachers who can't teach, we won't have enough money to recruit and retain teachers who can.

Education in America is greatly undermined by how difficult it is to get rid of bad teachers. And *Waiting for Superman* points the finger squarely at the teachers unions.

In the most infuriating scene in the movie, we are taken inside one of New York City's notorious "rubber rooms." We are shown a room filled with teachers sitting at desks; some are reading, some are sleeping, some are doing absolutely nothing. We are told that all of these teachers have been suspended for misconduct or incompetence. We are told that although these teachers have been banned from the classroom, their union contract prohibits them from being dismissed until they have had a hearing after a full investigation. We are told that this process takes months or even years, but that these suspended teachers can continue to collect their full salary and benefits by simply sitting in one of these "rubber rooms" during the working day.

The union and the city finally agreed to close the rubber rooms in 2010. At the time, rubber room teachers were costing the city $30 million per year—money that hence could not be used to pay teachers to actually teach. The closure of the rubber rooms, however, has not allowed that $30 million to be used to hire new teachers. The suspended teachers have largely been assigned to make-work jobs around the district, and some have been assigned to offices that have little or nothing for them to do. All the while, they continue to draw full salary and benefits (including the continued accrual of their pensions) while they await their hearings.[62]

Waiting for Superman makes the teachers unions look very bad, constantly opposing reforms, defending the status quo and protecting bad teachers. So who is this right-wing, union-bashing zealot that made *Waiting for Superman*? His name is Davis Guggenheim, and he's actually a left-wing, union-supporting zealot. He is best known for teaming with former Vice President Al Gore to make every liberal environmentalist's favorite film, *An Inconvenient Truth*.

Superman opens with Guggenheim recreating his daily drive past three public schools in order to drop his own kids off at a private school. Like a good liberal, he wants everyone to know that he's anguished about it: he feels like he's "betraying the ideals" he thought he lived by. He also wants everyone to know that he's anguished about taking on the teachers unions, because he's "a big believer in unions."[63]

But take on the teachers unions he does. According to *Variety*, Guggenheim's film makes "something of a foaming satanic beast out of Randi Weingarten, president of the American Federation of Teachers."[64] Liberal Dave's mom was a member of the AFT when she taught at Anne Beers. The AFT's late longtime president, the legendary Albert Shanker, is famously quoted as having said: "When school children start paying union dues, that's when I'll start representing the interests of school children."[65] Some latter day fans of Shanker now claim that there is insufficient evidence that he ever actually said that.[66] But there is also no evidence that Shanker ever denied making the statement, which has been publicly attributed to him countless times over many, many years. One would think that if Shanker did not make the statement and disagreed with it, he would have said so.

The quote attributed to Shanker is a statement of the obvious, controversial only because it bluntly expresses the "inconvenient truth" that teachers unions protect the interests of teachers, not school children. Even if Shanker did not really utter those words, it does not make them any less true. Union leaders often try to suggest that the interests of teachers are identical to the interests of school children. To which one might reply: Then why in the hell was New York City paying $30 million a year for rubber room teachers when poor kids desperately needed that money in the classroom?

The actor Matt Damon, like Liberal Dave (and ConservaDave), is the son of a schoolteacher. He was the keynote speaker at a 2011 rally in Washington, D.C. for Save Our Schools, an advocacy group that is endorsed by the teachers unions and many left-leaning organizations.[67] After the rally, a reporter and cameraman for Reason TV—the web channel for the libertarian think tank Reason Foundation—caught up with Damon. The reporter asked Damon about teacher tenure, a practice common in U.S. school systems whereby teachers, after a few years of service, attain a protected status that makes it very difficult and expensive to fire them. The reporter suggested that actors, because they do not have the job security of tenure, have more of an incentive to work harder and improve their craft. Why, asked the reporter, should it not be that way for teachers?

That really set Damon off. "So you think job insecurity is what makes me work hard?" Damon asked incredulously. The reporter started to elaborate, but Damon cut her off: "I want to be an actor. That's not an incentive. That's the thing. See, you take this MBA-style thinking, right? It's the problem with ed policy right now, this intrinsically paternalistic view of problems that are much more complex than that. It's like saying a teacher is going to get lazy when they have tenure. A teacher wants to teach. I mean, why else would you take a *sh*tty* salary and really long hours and do that job unless you really love to do it?"

The reporter's cameraman then asked Damon what we should do about the 10 percent of teachers who were not up to standard. Damon's mother, who was standing next to her famous son, asked the cameraman where he got that percentage. It is likely that 10 percent of the people in any profession are not up to standard, the cameraman replied.

"Well OK, but I mean, maybe you're a sh*tty cameraman, I don't know," retorted Damon.[68] You tell 'em, Matt!

But if that guy *had* been a sh*tty cameraman, Reason would have fired him. If that type of simple, common sense protection against sh*ttiness can be available for something as trivial as shooting videos for a libertarian think tank (with apologies to both the cameraman and the think tank), then why should it not be available to protect children—especially poor children—from the disastrous consequences of a bad education?

I have to hand it to Matt Damon. He sure sticks up for his mother's profession with more passion than I do. Damon's rant won him raves from many on the left. Michael Moore even suggested Damon run for President.[69] But the actor was off the mark for several reasons.

For one thing, U.S. public school teachers generally do not work long hours (especially those that get summers off!) and are not underpaid. Their salaries may be sh*tty compared to what movie stars make, but American teachers are among the highest paid teachers in the world.[70] And public school teachers earn substantially more than the market rate. We know that because public school teachers get paid much more than private school teachers, whose pay is determined by the market.[71]

What rang particularly hollow, though, was Damon's defense of a tenure system that protects bad teachers from getting fired. It's a great applause line to sing the praises of supposedly underpaid and overworked teachers. Most of us respond to that kind of bromide because we naturally sympathize with teachers, especially those of us who had some excellent teachers along the way (or whose mothers were teachers!). But good teachers don't need tenure, and bad ones don't deserve it. And more important than what the *teachers* deserve is that no *child* deserves a bad teacher. That is true whether the percentage of teachers who are substandard is 10 percent, one percent or 50 percent. Damon took offense to the suggestion that some teachers are not good at what they do. But it's obviously true, and to pretend otherwise is to simply put one's head in the sand at the expense of the school children. Matt Damon for President? He does not get ConservaDave's vote.

Damon's defense of tenure is typical of the type of rhetoric that teachers unions employ to protect their members from accountability. But the teachers unions don't rely primarily on rhetoric; they rely on raw political power. A 2010 study by the CATO Institute found that the two national teachers unions, the National Education Association and the aforementioned American Federation of Teachers, had together been "the most generous source of federal political donations over the past 20 years," contributing "roughly as much as Chevron, Exxon Mobile, the NRA, and Lockheed Martin combined." The AFT gave 99 percent of its money to Democrats during that period, the NEA 93 percent.[72] (One of the more surprising moments in *Waiting for Superman* was when liberal columnist Jonathan Alter admitted that the Democratic Party was a "wholly-owned subsidiary of the teachers unions.")

That same study found, however, that the teachers unions' federal political activity was dwarfed by their activity at the state and local level. That makes sense, because state governments and local school boards generally have a much more immediate impact on teachers than does the federal government. Teachers unions use their money and organization to help elect friendly (and mostly Democratic) state legislators, who in turn support laws that strengthen the unions' hand in contract negotiations. The unions also help elect friendly school board members. All of this creates a cozy, "fox guarding the hen house" relationship where the very elected officials who are in charge of negotiating with the teachers unions on behalf of the taxpayers are likely to be deeply indebted (politically speaking) to those unions. This tends to lead to more generous contracts, which enables the unions to raise more money, which enables them to keep those contributions flowing to their friends in office, which keeps the cycle repeating.

The teachers unions would suggest that we needn't be worried about their political power. After all, the teachers are the "good guys." They're fighting for more money for education, and in so doing they're fighting for the school children. This is a winning message for much of the electorate.

The problem is that the unions have traditionally been staunch enemies of the reforms that are desperately needed to rescue America's elementary and secondary educational system. Unions frequently offer proposals that are supposedly designed to improve education, but they consistently boil down to one thing: spend more money. If money were the determinant of success, then we'd have first place rankings in reading, math and science to match our first place ranking in spending. The problem is not that we don't spend enough, but that we don't spend wisely. We need more accountability for the money we spend on education—and that includes holding the teachers that we hire with that money accountable for their performance.

When unions and the rest of the public education establishment constantly demand more money for public schools, it's a little like a business telling its investors: "We need you to invest more money because we're wasting the money you've already invested, and therefore don't have enough money left over to do what we were supposed to do." Any sane investor would demand major changes as a condition to parting with more cash. Of course, that's the type of "MBA-style thinking" that, in Matt Damon's mind, has absolutely no place in the debate over "ed policy." The unions are fortunate because when they make their pitch for more money, they're not dealing with private investors who have their own money at stake. They're dealing with a much more sympathetic audience: friendly politicians who owe their positions to the unions—and it is other people's money that's at stake. And for the benefit of the public that's listening in, they get to add a little hostage-taking language to the end of their pitch: "If you don't give us the money, the kids will be hurt." Major changes as a condition to parting with more cash? Fugetaboutit!

Teachers unions have been enemies of common sense. Common sense tells us that we need to make it easier to fire bad teachers, as *Waiting for Superman* illustrated. Common sense tells us that we need a greater ability to reward good teachers if we want to keep them. Common sense tells us that smart and talented teachers will leave the profession if they can't be paid more than their less accomplished colleagues, and that this will drive down the overall quality of the talent pool. The unions have consistently fought against tenure reform and "merit pay" arrangements that allow good teachers to be paid more than bad ones.

When it becomes politically untenable for unions to continue to thwart reforms that are popular with the public, the unions sometimes belatedly embrace those reforms—but then work to limit their impact. For example, local unions might acquiesce to merit pay but then work to narrow the pay differential between good and bad teachers. Or they might claim to welcome the competition from charter schools, but then work to limit their funding, put a cap on the number of charter schools that can operate, and impose as many rules and regulations upon them as possible.

The reforms that the teachers unions fear most are "school choice" programs where parents are granted vouchers to send their children to the school of their choice—public or private, religious or secular. Nobel Laureate Milton Friedman first advocated vouchers as a way of fixing our educational system in the 1950s.[73] As Friedman conceived it, every student's parents would get a voucher of a certain dollar value. The parents could use the voucher to send their child to public school at no additional cost, or could send their child to the private school of their choice and apply the value of the voucher against the tuition bill. The money would follow the child: if the child went to public school, the public school system would get the amount of his voucher; if the child went to private school, the private school would get the money.

Friedman's idea was that all elementary and secondary students would get vouchers. Public schools would no longer have a monopoly on public funding for education. They would have to compete with private schools to attract those public funds by convincing parents to entrust them with their children's education. Competition, as it does in other fields, would spur innovation that would improve both public and private schools. Public schools in particular would feel competitive pressure to get more money into the classroom, which would require them to trim their wasteful administrative budgets.

A variation of Friedman's idea is to provide vouchers only to those who need them the most: the poor. The idea is that parents who can afford to send their children to private school—even if it requires great sacrifice—already have school choice. The parents who really need help are those who absolutely cannot afford to move their children into private schools. Failing inner city school systems can afford to ignore the needs of children whose parents cannot afford to "take their business elsewhere." They cannot, however, ignore the needs of powerful adult special interest groups such as the unions. The teachers unions want to protect their members from accountability for their performance, and the unions for other employees want to keep their members on school payrolls whether or not they're needed for the children's education. That type of dynamic, where all of the stakeholders have power except the children and their parents, is what caused the tragic deterioration of the D.C. public school system and others like it. Vouchers alter that dynamic, empowering poor parents to act as consumers and demand that schools be responsive to their children's needs. This not only liberates poor children from the captivity of failing schools, it puts competitive pressure on those failing schools to improve.

For teachers unions, vouchers are Public Enemy Number 1. They complain that these programs deprive public schools of money that they need, which can only impede their efforts to improve. It is true that when a child transfers out of public school under a voucher program his voucher money goes with him—but then the school is relieved of the cost of having to educate that child. A voucher is almost always worth less than the cost of educating a child in public school, so money is saved when a student uses a voucher to attend private school.

More importantly, though, the union argument loses sight of the fundamental issue: Taxpayers fund elementary and secondary education for the purpose of educating children, not for the purpose of supporting the public school system. Supporting public schools is a means to an end, not an end in itself—and not the only means to that end. Support for the public school system—and the adults who are employed by that system—should never take priority over the underlying goal of educating the children.

Columnist Shikha Dalmia, in a piece criticizing the Save Our Schools (SOS) movement and Matt Damon's support thereof, explains the merits of vouchers with an interesting analogy: "[A]ll that school choice proponents want to do is use the existing funds to transform public education from a soup-kitchen to a food-stamp welfare model, to put it in non-MBA terms that Damon understands," wrote Dalmia. "Just as the hungry have no control over the gruel they are offered at soup kitchens, parents have no real control over what their kids are served up in public schools. And just as food stamps empower the poor to shop at stores best serving their grocery needs, vouchers empower parents to choose schools that best meet their children's needs. No one would consider it progress if, prodded by soup-kitchen unions, we eliminated food stamps and opened more soup kitchens. Yet that's what passes for enlightened thinking among SOS 'progressives.'"[74]

Defenders of the status quo often argue that if we give poor parents vouchers, they'll be taken advantage of by shady, fly-by-night schools that are just out for a quick buck. Boy, talk about an "intrinsically paternalistic view," as Matt Damon would put it. Yes, some parents may make mistakes—but vouchers will allow them to correct those mistakes. Should poor kids be trapped forever in failed public schools because of the risk that they may temporarily end up in private schools that don't live up to their billing? Should we force poor people to eat gruel at soup kitchens because of the risk that they might use food stamps to buy junk food?

Some argue that voucher programs violate the constitutional separation of church and state unless they exclude parochial schools. If that were the case, then Pell Grants for low-income college students would also be unconstitutional. Liberal Dave used his Pell Grants to attend the University of Pennsylvania—but he also could have used them at Yeshiva University, Notre Dame, Georgetown or any other religious university. This is an important issue because Catholic schools, in particular, have proven to be very effective at educating inner city students at a fraction of the cost of public schools.

Teachers unions throw out all sorts of reasons to oppose school choice, but here's the real reason they hate it: School choice threatens their power. They want the public money to continue to flow exclusively into the public school system, where they can exercise a great deal of influence by cultivating friendly politicians. They hate charter schools because those schools get to escape the bureaucratic straight jacket that the unions have so painstakingly constructed over the years to protect their members. However, the unions sometimes feel forced to publicly embrace charter schools— if only to show that they're not just inflexible zealots who mindlessly defend the status quo at all costs. As threatening as charter schools are to the unions, they're much preferable to voucher programs. At least charter schools are still part of the public school system, so the unions can wield their influence to keep them in check. With vouchers—true school choice—money starts to flow outside of the system, where it becomes impossible for the unions to control. That's why unions are sometimes willing to support charter schools as a way of heading off public demand for true school choice.

The unions' intrinsic interest in perpetuating the dominance of traditional public schools, which they can more easily control, causes them to oppose reforms that will give parents—especially poor parents—more options. It's not that union members have a conscious desire to restrict the options of poor parents; it's just that the additional options—be they charter schools or true school choice programs—necessarily erode the unions' power. But for poor parents whose children are stuck in failing schools, additional options are what they need more than anything else. Sure, poor parents can vocally support measures to reform the public school system from within, such as merit pay and tenure reform. But those parents will never have the power to compete with the wealthy unions—unless the parents are endowed with the power that all consumers have, the power to take their business elsewhere. Options are power. Public schools will reform themselves when they are forced to do so to prevent a mass exodus of students—and money— from their system.

There is much that can be done to improve our schools, especially for the children who need a good education to overcome the disadvantages of their birth. Tenure should be abolished for elementary and secondary school teachers. If it isn't abolished, it should at the very least be reformed so that tenure is only granted to excellent teachers and does not significantly impede firing teachers who need to be fired. The pay scale should not merely reward teachers for longevity; it should incentivize every teacher to strive for excellence. These and other reforms will happen if public schools are forced to compete for the loyalty of parents, forced to treat them as customers. The political process has proven itself completely ineffective to control the wasteful bureaucracy that burdens public education; only market competition can provide the discipline to squeeze out the dead weight.

The more choice that parents have, the better. More choice leads to more competition, which leads to more innovation and more discipline. Charter schools are good, and we should resist efforts by teachers unions to limit them, defund them and shackle them. True school choice, with vouchers that can be used in public or private schools, is even better. Let all different types of organizations open schools—charter or private—and join the effort to ensure that every child can get a great education. Nonprofits, for-profits, religious organizations, unions—let them all participate in a vibrant market. The more the merrier.

Davis Guggenheim was and is a committed liberal. But he had the intellectual honesty to see, at least in the area of education, that liberal *policies* were not the best way to achieve liberal *ideals*. Policies are just means to an end; it is the ideals that matter. The most important liberal ideal about education is that it should be a means to give every child in our society, no matter how poor, the opportunity to succeed. And the best way to achieve this ideal is through the conservative policies of competition and choice.

7 NURSING OUR HEALTH CARE SYSTEM BACK TO HEALTH

It was an historic day indeed. On March 23, 2010, President Barack Obama signed the Patient Protection and Affordable Care Act, a bill to comprehensively reform America's health care system. It was the culmination not only of a year-long legislative battle, but of almost a century of efforts to create a national health care system through federal legislation.

National health care has long been a dream of liberal Democrats, but the historical legacy of Obama's legislative victory actually reaches back to Theodore Roosevelt. The former Republican President campaigned for national health insurance during his 1912 run for President. Roosevelt was not running as a Republican in 1912; he had formed his own breakaway Bull Moose Party after a rift within the GOP. Regardless of what he was running as, he lost, and his health insurance proposal went nowhere.

A succession of Democratic Presidents picked up the torch for national health care, but their proposals, alas, also went nowhere. National health insurance was left out of President Franklin D. Roosevelt's New Deal legislation in the 1930s, presumably because of stiff opposition from the American Medical Association. In the 1940s, President Harry Truman proposed a national health care plan that included mandatory coverage for all Americans. The American Medical Association continued to oppose calls for national health care, and Truman's plan died in Congress. President Lyndon B. Johnson succeeded in establishing national health care programs for the most vulnerable Americans—Medicare for the elderly and Medicaid for the poor. Candidate Jimmy Carter renewed the call for a national health insurance system with universal and mandatory coverage. He backed off on that once he was elected president, citing the weak economy. President Bill Clinton appointed his First Lady, Hillary Clinton, to develop a proposal for universal coverage. In a major blow to Clinton's presidency, "HillaryCare" crashed and burned in Congress.[75]

All of that sad history seemed to melt away when the Patient Protection and Affordable Care Act was finally signed into law. As he watched the signing ceremony live on television, Liberal Dave caught a tear of joy running down his cheek.

To be sure, getting there hadn't been pretty. Not a single Republican had voted for the bill,[76] and the Democrats had to resort to some highly controversial parliamentary maneuvers to get it passed.[77] But none of that dampened the supporters' jubilation in the wake of the bill's passage.

Democratic Congressman James Clyburn of South Carolina called the health care bill "the Civil Rights Act of the 21st century."

President Obama marked the occasion with lofty rhetoric: "In the end what this day represents is another stone firmly laid in the foundation of the American dream," he said. "Tonight, we answered the call of history as so many generations of Americans have before us. When faced with crisis, we did not shrink from our challenges. We overcame them. We did not avoid our responsibilities, we embraced it. We did not fear our future, we shaped it."[78]

But perhaps Vice President Joseph Biden put it best when the microphone overheard him tossing this bouquet to his boss: "Mr.

President, this is a big f***ing deal."[79] Indeed it was, Joe. Indeed it was.

Although the health care debate had been deeply divisive, Republicans as well as Democrats believed that health care reform was necessary. In 2009, there were 50.7 million people in the U.S. without health insurance, or 16.7 percent of the population.[80] According to World Health Organization statistics from 2006, the U.S. spent more on health care per capita than any other country. Health care expenditures in the U.S. were 15.3 percent of U.S. gross domestic product that year, the second highest percentage in the world.[81] Both Liberal Dave and ConservaDave generally agreed that health care in the U.S needed to be more accessible and more affordable, without compromising quality.

So what exactly was in the Patient Protection and Affordable Care Act, and in a companion bill called the Health Care and Reconciliation Act of 2010? Plenty, actually. So much that it seems implausible that many members of Congress actually read the bills as they were rushed to passage. The two bills, which many collectively refer to as "Obamacare," had a combined page count of over 2,800 pages.[82] Then-Speaker of the House Nancy Pelosi famously said prior to the House vote that "we have to pass the bill so that you can find out what is in it," thus bringing a creative sense of dyslexia to the concepts of transparency and good governance.[83]

Now that Obamacare has been passed and signed into law, we are at liberty to reveal what was in it. In 2012, a divided Supreme Court ruled that most of the provisions of Obamacare are constitutional. Republicans, however, have vowed to repeal and replace Obamacare if they regain the White House and sufficient control of Congress. It is thus not certain that Obamacare, which is scheduled to be phased in through 2018, will ever be fully implemented. In light of this uncertainty, this chapter will discuss what Obamacare "would" do rather than what it "will" do. Whether or not it survives in its original form, though, Obamacare needs to be studied. It is an excellent case study of the mindset of those who believe that the way to solve any problem is to put the Politicrats (as ConservaDave would call them) in control. And it is a cautionary tale for people like Liberal Dave about how well intentioned government programs can end up hurting the very people they are designed to help. The lessons we can learn from studying Obamacare can be applied to almost any major policy initiative that we might consider in the future.

Here, then, are some of the basics of Obamacare:[84]

Individual Mandate to Buy Health Insurance: Everyone not otherwise covered through their employer, the government or otherwise would be required to purchase health insurance. That insurance would have to meet minimum standards set by the government. Those who didn't purchase insurance would be fined, with some exemptions for people with low incomes.

Employer Mandate to Provide Health Insurance: Every business that employed 50 or more workers generally would have to provide health insurance to its employees. Those who did not would have to pay a penalty. Employers would also have to pay a penalty if they offered insurance but required employees to pay too much of the cost of that insurance.

Federal Restrictions on How Much Money Insurance Companies Could Make: Insurance companies, which have traditionally been regulated by the states, would be subject to comprehensive federal rules telling them what they could and could not do. A specified percentage of the premiums each insurance company collected would have to be paid out in benefits.

No Consideration of Pre-Existing Conditions: Insurance companies would no longer be allowed to deny coverage to applicants for being in bad health, for having a medical condition, or otherwise on account of claims experience, medical history or disability.

Benefits for "Adult Children": Insurance companies would be required to allow parents to keep their dependent children on their policies until the age of 26.

"Rescission" Curtailed: Insurance companies would no longer be able to cancel policies because the policyholder's statements in the original insurance application were later found to have been inaccurate, unless the policyholder had committed fraud or intentionally misstated a material fact.

"Lifetime Limits" Abolished: Insurers would be prohibited from imposing a limit on the total amount of benefits that could be paid out over the life of a policy.

"Free" Preventive Care: Insurers would be required to cover a wide range of preventive care services at "no cost."

Restricted Ability to Charge Higher Premiums to Riskier Customers: Insurers would not be allowed to charge unhealthy people higher premiums than healthy people. Their ability to charge older people higher premiums than younger people (who tend to be in better health) would be limited. Their ability to charge smokers higher premiums than non-smokers would also be limited.

Subsidies: Medicaid, the government health program for the poor, would be expanded to cover everyone with an income less than 133 percent of the poverty level. For people not eligible for Medicaid but with incomes less than four times the poverty level, the federal government would subsidize their health insurance.

Exchanges: States would set up their own "exchanges"—insurance marketplaces for people who don't get their insurance through an employer or the government. The exchanges would be clearinghouses where people wishing to buy insurance would be matched up with insurance companies wishing to sell policies. Policies offered through the exchanges would be required to offer minimum benefits prescribed by the federal government.

Long-term Care: A long-term care program was supposed to be established as part of Obamacare. The Community Living

Assistance and Support Act (CLASS Act) provided for a supposedly self-financed program to provide in-home caretakers and adult day care to seniors and the disabled. More on this later....

All told, Obamacare would result in unprecedented federal involvement in health care. It was clearly a big, ahem, deal, as Vice President Biden observed. But was it a good deal?

One important issue (at least to some people) is how much Obamacare would cost. According to the Congressional Budget Office's initial projections, Obamacare would actually *reduce* the budget deficit—by $138 billion over 10 years.[85] That sounded like great news, almost like learning that we could eat all the chocolate cake we wanted and never get fat. Perhaps they should have made Obamacare even bigger so we could have saved even more.

Before you break out the confetti, consider the sobering truth about entitlement programs. An entitlement program, as the name suggests, *entitles* people who meet certain requirements to receive certain payments from the government. The actual cost of such a program is therefore not determined by a fixed budget, but by the number of people who actually end up meeting the requirements and claiming the entitlement. Oh, and don't forget to add in the people who don't meet the requirements but successfully secure entitlement payments through fraud or error.

This leads us to ConservaDave's three rules about government entitlement programs: (1) the cost of an entitlement program is determined by how and how much it is actually used (and abused), even if the cost estimates are wrong; (2) the cost estimates are always wrong; (3) "wrong" always means way too low.[86] In 1967, a House committee projected that Medicare would cost $12 billion in 1990; the actual cost was *more than eight times higher*, just shy of $100 billion. In 1987, Congress estimated that special relief payments to hospitals under Medicaid would total under $1 billion in 1992; the actual cost was $17 billion, *over 17 times higher than the projection made just five years earlier.* Gross underestimations like this are not the exception; they are the rule.[87]

Entitlement programs have inherent qualities that make them almost impossible to control. People figure out how to maximize the money they can extract from the programs. It's not so much the average folks who do this (although some of them become very well versed on how to benefit from the system), but rather the professionals—doctors, hospital administrators, etc.—who must constantly deal with the programs in the course of their business. As for the average folks, they become dependent on the programs—to the point where they get highly agitated when anyone so much as suggests that we need to get the cost of these programs under control. It's not for nothing that Social Security is called the "third rail of American politics"—if you touch it, you die. ("Third rail" is a reference to the highly electrified—and hence highly deadly—rails that run parallel to subway tracks to supply the trains with power.) And it's a rare politician who is willing to incur the wrath of senior citizens by suggesting reforms to Medicare.

When entitlement programs are established, they instantly attain the presumption of permanence. In federal budget parlance, spending on entitlement programs is designated as "mandatory spending"—as if suggesting reductions to that spending would be contrary to law, morality or the natural order.

While the political will to cut entitlements is usually nonexistent, the political pressure to expand existing entitlements is often overwhelming. Once a program is established, it becomes a "placeholder" for people who will naturally want to expand it: the activists who supported the program, the professionals who receive revenues from it, the bureaucrats who gain power and prestige from administering it, the lobbyists who pushed for it, the members of Congress who championed it, the people who get benefits from it, and the people who narrowly miss the eligibility requirements and want in. The program's initial supporters invariably had wanted it to be bigger, but settled for what they could get—for the time being. Once the heavy lifting of establishing a new program has been completed, expanding it becomes simple by comparison—and the program will have a natural constituency that will be constantly looking for opportunities to do just that.

The State Children's Health Insurance Program (SCHIP), for example, was estimated to cost $5 billion per year when it was established in 1997. Congress has been supplementing the SCHIP budget with hundreds of millions of additional dollars each year. President Obama, during his first month in office, signed a $33 billion bill to add 4 million additional children to the program.[88]

Obamacare would be the largest new federal entitlement program since Medicare and Medicaid were created in 1965. Does it really pass the laugh test to suggest that Obamacare would reduce the deficit? A CATO Institute study pokes through all of the accounting gimmicks and rigged assumptions that allowed the Congressional Budget Office to conclude that Obamacare would "only" cost $875 billion over its first 10 years. CATO concludes that the bill would likely cost over three times that much in its first 10 years—over $2.7 trillion—and would add $823 billion to the national debt. Furthermore, CATO points to estimates suggesting that the fiscal damage done by Obamacare would be even worse in its second 10 years, possibly adding another $1.5 trillion to the deficit. And further-furthermore, CATO roughly estimates that if the Congressional Budget Office had evaluated Obamacare under the same rules that they used to evaluate President Clinton's failed health care plan—that is, accounting for all of the hidden costs that the bill would shift from the federal government to individuals, businesses and the states—the true cost of Obamacare would likely approximate $7 trillion.[89]

So would Obamacare reduce the deficit, or explode it to terrifying proportions? For the average voter, it's hard to know whom to believe: the scholars at the CATO Institute, or the people who are telling us that we can eat all the chocolate cake we want and never get fat. As much as I love chocolate cake, it may be more prudent in this case to vote with my brain and not with my stomach.

The CATO study was prepared *before* a bad piece of news came out about Obamacare. The CLASS Act, the supposedly self-sustaining long-term care program for seniors, was abandoned by Obama's Department of Health and Human Services in October 2011—before it was even started—because they could not find a way to make it actuarially sound. In fact, the CLASS Act was supposed to have been *more than* self-sustaining: it was supposed to have generated net revenues, accounting for more than half of the supposed deficit reduction that Obamacare was officially projected to achieve over 10 years.

The fatal flaws in the CLASS Act were caught early. That is not because the bureaucrats at the Department of Health and Human Services were proactive or had a sudden bout of conscience. It is because the law specifically required the CLASS Act program to be actuarially sound, which forced the bureaucrats to perform the analysis which led them to discover that it could not be. The actuarial soundness requirement was slipped into the CLASS Act by then-Senator Judd Gregg (R-New Hampshire), who had this reaction to the program's demise: "Had the whole bill been subject to the accounting and actuarial review that the CLASS Act was, it would not have survived either."[90]

Now let's think about this: How likely is it that the CLASS Act was the *only* feature of Obamacare that could not live up to its rosy projections? Might the 2,800 pages of Obamacare be chock full of other hidden gems that are bursting with costly, unintended consequences?

The sad truth is that massive government programs *always* bring unintended consequences. Newton's third law of motion states that for every action there is always an equal and opposite reaction. This law applies to public policy as well, and it only stands to reason that

2,800 pages of action would trigger a mind-boggling number of equal and opposite reactions—many of them unanticipated, unintended, undesired and unfunded.

The people who designed Social Security did not foresee the drop in fertility and increase in longevity that is requiring fewer and fewer workers to support more and more retirees. The people who designed Medicare did not foresee that longer life-spans resulting from more affordable medical care (good) would cause costs to go through the roof (bad). And nor was it intended that the popularity of these programs would make it politically almost impossible to reform them as actuarial flaws came to light.

An entire book could be written about the unintended consequences of Obamacare. In fact, an entire book *has* been written about the unintended consequences of Obamacare.[91] That book notes that an estimated 159 new agencies, boards, commissions and offices would be created to implement Obamacare—"estimated" because the law gives the executive branch the ability to create even more agencies without Congress's approval.[92] The creation of a new bureaucracy of that size would inevitably result in a very important unintended consequence: health care would become the subject of a lobbying frenzy more intense than has ever been seen even for that industry. The more you expand the power of government in a particular area, the more you create a demand for lobbyists in that area—and the more you increase the risk that the Politicrats will play favorites in ways that the public will never be able to detect. Lobbyists would be swarming like locusts around each of those 159 new bureaucratic bodies, trying to influence who gets appointed to them and what policies they promulgate. An unprecedented amount of power over health care would be concentrated in this new bureaucracy and in the political types appointed to oversee it. The need to stay on the good side of this bureaucracy would inspire a flood of political contributions. Health care would become more politicized than ever.

The politicization was already well underway when the bill was just starting to be phased in. By October 2011, the Obama Administration's Department of Health and Human Services had already granted waivers from a key provision of Obamacare to approximately 1,800 companies, unions and even entire states.[93] That key provision, to be phased in in stages, would eventually prohibit employers from offering insurance policies that placed a limit on the amount of benefits that could be paid out every year. The theory was that an employee should not have coverage that could get "used up" in any given year, requiring the employee to pay the excess. That's a great theory, until you consider the unintended consequences. The provision would pretty much destroy the market for "mini-med" policies, which feature low premiums in exchange for limits on annual payouts. But it simply isn't economical for many employers to offer part-time, seasonal and other low-wage workers insurance other than "mini-med" policies; these employees don't contribute enough to the bottom line to justify the added expense. Without these policies, many employers could not afford to offer *any* health insurance to these employees. The employees would either be forced into the notorious Medicaid program or be left to purchase much more expensive insurance on their own. The Obama Administration was therefore forced to grant all of these waivers, covering millions of employees,[94] in order to prevent these employees from losing their health insurance.

Columnist Milton Wolf assailed the large number of waivers as "a tacit admission that Obamacare is a failure." Writing in May 2011, when the number of waivers granted had only reached 1, 372, Wolf noted: "More than 50 percent of the Obamacare waiver beneficiaries are union members, which is striking because union members account for less than 12 percent of the American work force. The same unions that provided more than $120 million to Democrats in the last two elections and, in many cases, openly campaigned in favor of the government takeover of your health care, now celebrate that Obamacare is not their problem."[95]

Wolf's column raises the very troubling possibility that politics had some influence over who has gotten waivers and who hasn't. "Why did these particular businesses receive waivers?" asked Wolf in his column. "The administration that calls itself the most transparent in history won't say. Nor will it explain why it has denied at least 79 requests from others." In addition to the many Obama-supporting unions that have been granted waivers, other beneficiaries have included the AARP (the powerful lobbying group for senior citizens that actively campaigned for Obamacare) and the entire state of Nevada (whose Senator, Majority Leader Harry Reid, was instrumental in ensuring that Obamacare got passed). In May 2011, 20 percent of the waivers granted were to businesses located in the area represented by former Speaker of the House Nancy Pelosi, who was also instrumental in ensuring that Obamacare got passed.[96] Even if politics played no role in the granting of any of these waivers, it is quite damning that so many Obamacare supporters successfully exempted themselves from rules that they strongly advocated for the rest of the country. And it is quite troubling that Politicrats have had such broad discretion to decide who got these waivers and who didn't. The potential for favoritism, extortion and abuse under such an arrangement is frightening.

The "no limits on benefits" requirement is one of the many features of Obamacare that sounds great until you consider the costs and unintended consequences. You could string these goodies together into a very pleasing narrative: Your employer will have to provide you with insurance. The amount that you have to contribute to that insurance will be limited to what you can afford. You can't be turned down because of a pre-existing condition, and they won't be able to charge you more because you're in bad health. They can charge you more if you're older—but only to a limit. They can charge you more if you smoke—but again, only to a limit. If you get sick, your benefits will never run out, and your insurance company won't be able to cancel your coverage because of mistakes in your application. You can keep your children on your plan until they're 26. We'll limit what those greedy insurance companies can make, to make sure that they have more money to pay benefits to you. And you'll get preventive care absolutely free!

What's not to like about any of that? Plenty, actually, when you consider that each of these goodies has a cost attached to it, and that it is impossible to keep the burdens associated with these costs from spilling over and inflicting collateral damage on those who are supposed to benefit.

At least one expert believes that the passage of Obamacare stopped the economic recovery in its tracks.[97] The mandates that Obamacare put on employers raised the cost of hiring workers. And, since many of the important details of Obamacare would be filled in by hundreds of thousands of pages of regulations that would be written by bureaucrats in the future, hiring workers in the meantime would eventually trigger additional costs that could not yet be known. Businesses with less than 50 workers would be exempted from some of Obamacare's expensive mandates—and hence would have a strong disincentive to hire more workers once they reached that threshold. With all of these disincentives to create jobs, Obamacare has already made life particularly difficult for people who desperately need to find work.

The CATO Institute study points to several other unintended consequences of Obamacare, including this one: "The new insurance regulations may result in many insurers withdrawing from their less profitable markets, leaving many consumers with few insurance choices. Already, Principal Financial has stopped selling health insurance, which has resulted in coverage being dropped for some 840,000 people. And Aetna has announced that it is pulling out of the individual market in Colorado. Perversely, the Patient

Protection and Affordable Care Act could reduce competition in the insurance market."[98]

The prohibition against insurance companies considering pre-existing conditions backfired immediately. That prohibition went into effect for children in 2010, and would be expanded to cover adults in 2014. As soon as the rule went into effect for children, several major health insurers stopped issuing "child-only" health insurance policies. The concern was that parents would wait to buy coverage until their child needed treatment (after all, the child could not be turned down because of the pre-existing condition) and then cancel the policy as soon as the treatment was finished.[99] Thus, a rule intended to make it easier for children to be covered by health insurance has actually made it harder.

There is much concern about what would happen in 2014 if Obamacare is not overturned. That is the year that insurers would no longer be allowed to deny adults coverage because of pre-existing conditions. Healthy adults might "game the system" by not buying coverage until they need care, and then cancelling the coverage as soon as they no longer need the care. These people would of course be fined for not complying with the individual mandate to buy insurance. However, healthy adults may find it more economical to pay the fine than to purchase insurance that they don't yet feel they need. This phenomenon could potentially be very costly to insurance companies and cause a further contraction in the industry. That would reduce price competition and leave consumers with fewer options.

Problems have also arisen with the provision allowing parents to keep dependent children on their plans until the age of 26. Each dependent increases insurance premiums by thousands of dollars,[100] and employers have started restricting the dependent coverage they offer so they could avoid bearing these costs.[101]

Another consequence of all of the new and impending burdens that Obamacare places on insurance companies is that premiums have shot up considerably since the law was passed.[102] This is no doubt a consequence of all of the "free" benefits that insurance companies are forced to provide us under Obamacare. Of course, the people who can least afford these price hikes are the very people that Obamacare was intended to help the most.

While all of the negative consequences discussed above have been unintended, they were hardly unforeseeable. They are classic illustrations of what happens when government tries to control too much. And they all started to arise when our adventure with Obamacare was barely underway.

The way the Politicrats designed Obamacare reminds me of a never-ending game of Whac-A-Mole. For the uninitiated, Whac-A-Mole is a game where little plastic moles pop randomly out of various holes, and the object is to whack them back down into their holes with a toy mallet. Only in the Obamacare version of Whac-A-Mole, the "mole-popping" isn't as random: the very act of whacking one mole is what causes the next mole to pop up somewhere else. The other difference is that in the Obamacare version, the game never ends. Up pops the first mole: sick people can't get insurance. No problem: just force insurance companies to cover pre-existing conditions. Whack! But look over there, another mole just popped up: covering pre-existing conditions would cause insurance companies to lose a lot of money and drive them out of business. No problem: just raise premiums on healthy people and also sell more insurance to people who didn't previously have it. Whack! But another mole just popped up: if insurance companies have to cover pre-existing conditions, then healthy people won't buy insurance until they need treatment and will cancel it as soon as the treatment is over. No problem: just force everyone to buy insurance immediately and fine them if they don't. Whack! But another mole just popped up....[103] Before you know it, you're up to 2,800 pages of legislation—with hundreds of thousands of pages of regulations yet to come.

136

By greatly expanding the government's role in health care, we have chosen to become more like Europe at a time when not even Europe can afford to be like Europe. The European social welfare state model cannot be sustained over the long run. Proponents of Obamacare have typically been big fans of Western European and Canadian health care. While systems vary from country to country, most of those countries face serious problems. Tight government control of the health care market, designed to make health care more affordable, has perverse side-effects: When most or all of the money spent on health care is determined by government, price controls must be imposed on the market to keep health care affordable for the people (and to keep the government's obligations from getting way out of control). These price controls, which are designed by bureaucrats and override the free market, artificially limit what doctors can earn. Over time, this tends to create a shortage of doctors. Other shortages can result as well: medications, supplies, medical devices, hospitals, clinics—all of the personnel, goods, services and infrastructure required to deliver health care. When health care is "affordable" to all but there is no market mechanism to ensure an adequate supply of doctors, medications, hospitals, etc., the only solution is to ration care. Rationing can take the form of long waits that can sometimes be life-threatening, or withholding certain treatments outright because bureaucrats decide they're not "cost effective." Also, there is less financial incentive to produce innovations in drugs, medical devices and treatments, so less innovation occurs.

Some of these countries do a better job at addressing these problems than others—using their own versions of "Whac-A-Mole"—but it comes at quite a cost that cannot be sustained in the long run. Much of that cost is borne by the U.S.: countries under the U.S. defense umbrella can get away with spending minimal amounts on defense, which frees up their resources to support health care and other entitlement programs. But the massive welfare states that these countries have constructed still demand high levels of taxation, which depress economic growth. And even that's not enough: in order to provide lavish benefits to their people today, these welfare states must mortgage their children's future through excessive levels of borrowing. And because these levels of borrowing are not sustainable in the long run, the social welfare states themselves are not sustainable in the long run.

The American system, for all its faults, is the one that attracts the best doctors and spurs the most innovation. America is still the place where people from those other countries want to come if they really get sick. America thus serves as a "safety valve" for many who are living under socialized medicine—providing medical innovations that benefit the entire world, and, for those who can afford it, timely treatment not possible in their home countries because of rationing.

Europe is showing us how painful it is to reform a bloated welfare state. The most daunting obstacle becomes the sense of entitlement that corrodes the character of the people after generations of relying upon the government for their every need. French workers, who are guaranteed long vacations and enjoy almost insurmountable protections against lay-offs, staged widespread riots in 2010 to protest the raising of the retirement age—from 60 to 62.[104] And since rioting is a physically demanding activity—it takes a lot of vigor to throw bottles, break windows, charge at police barricades and the like—one would presume that most of the rioters were nowhere near the retirement age. Riots have become routine in Greece, which has been forced to scale back its extravagant welfare state because international lenders are no longer willing to fund it.

Obamacare is not European-style socialized medicine, but it would move us dangerously in that direction in ways that could irrevocably damage our national character. Obamacare doesn't just focus on helping the people who really need help; it would completely restructure health care for all of us. By attempting to give "goodies" not only to the poor but to the middle class as well, Obamacare seeks to create a broad constituency to keep the new system in place. The hope—or danger, from my perspective—is that people would become so attached to their government-mandated benefits and public subsidies that they would become afraid to ever give them up—even if they were locked into a system that provided mediocre care. Under that scenario, the entire health care system would come to resemble Medicare: it would be heavily controlled by government, it would lock us indefinitely into unsustainable long-term financial commitments, and a majority of the electorate would fight any reforms or cutbacks just as vigorously as seniors fight to defend Medicare. Heaven help us if we ever get to that point. Heaven help us if we ever become like some in Europe have become—so hopelessly addicted to keeping our own state benefits flowing that we completely forget about the burden we're placing on our children and grandchildren.

So if not Obamacare, then what? How can we make health care more affordable, more responsive to our needs, and accessible to all? The answer invokes the very same principles that are needed to save public education: transfer power away from the bureaucracies by empowering people to be consumers. An excellent book entitled *Why Obamacare is Wrong for America* offers tangible ideas on how to do that, and the discussion that follows borrows liberally from that work.[105]

Let's start by recognizing that most Americans are largely insulated from the cost implications of their health care decisions. When we buy something with money out of our own pocket, we have the incentive to make sure we're getting good value for the price. This is especially true for major purchases. With a car, for example, we might decline some of the costly options if we don't think they're worth the extra money. With health care, there's usually a major disconnect between the services we use and the immediate impact on our wallet. This is certainly true for people whose health coverage is provided by the government through programs such as Medicare and Medicaid, but it is also largely true for people who have private insurance.

It is very common for people to get their insurance through their employer, and that's no accident. The federal government has for many years subsidized employer-provided insurance through tax breaks. Why have we given tax breaks for employer-provided insurance but not for insurance that individuals buy on their own? There's no economic reason; we just started doing it that way many years ago and never stopped. Employees generally don't think about the fact that what employers spend on health insurance keeps salaries lower. People tend to consider employer contributions to their insurance as "free stuff," and tend not to perceive an incentive to be as vigilant about health care costs as they are about things they buy directly. This suggests that market discipline over prices is weaker in health care than it is in other industries, which helps explain why health care costs have been rising so much faster than general inflation.[106] This inevitably holds wages down, because employers who have to spend more on health insurance have less money left over for salary.

The authors of *Why Obamacare is Wrong for America* propose granting people a subsidy to buy health insurance and health care services. People who do not purchase health insurance would lose the entire value of the subsidy.[107] The subsidy could take the form of a voucher or a tax credit. If in the form of a tax credit, it would be "refundable"—that is, if your tax liability is less than the value of the credit, you would get the difference in the form of a voucher.

There are various ways that the amounts of the subsidies could be set. The guiding principles should be that every American be able to afford health insurance, and that every American have a strong incentive to buy it.

The subsidy could be paid for, at least in part, by eliminating the tax breaks for employer-provided health insurance. The old employer-based system would be replaced by one where people would have a much wider range of options to satisfy their particular needs, and a strong incentive to make sure they're getting the best value for their money. Your insurance options would no longer be dictated by whatever your employer happened to offer, and you wouldn't lose your insurance if you lost your job. Most importantly, however, Americans would approach health insurance as active consumers, concerned about price and value, rather than as passive recipients. This would bring a healthy dose of competition to health insurance and health care and help keep prices down.

Additional competition should be provided by allowing insurance to be sold across state lines. Competition in the health insurance market is blocked by state laws that only allow a small number of insurers to sell policies within the state. These artificial barriers to competition limit choice and keep prices high. In the health insurance industry, everyone should be allowed to compete with everyone else. A robust, competitive market is the best way to control costs.

Massive damage awards against doctors in medical malpractice cases also drive up health care costs. Victims of medical malpractice should of course be compensated for their injuries, but sympathetic juries often go beyond that and award damages for intangible pain and suffering as well as punitive damages. Punitive damages in malpractice cases are amounts awarded to victims for the purpose of punishing doctors for particularly egregious behavior. They are awarded on top of compensatory damages, which compensate victims for economic losses resulting from malpractice—hospital bills, lost wages and the like. The prevalence of large jury awards, typically featuring hefty punitive damages and generous compensation for pain and suffering, drives up the malpractice insurance premiums that doctors have to pay. This, of course, gets passed on to patients and insurance companies and raises the cost of medical care. More importantly, the risk of potentially ruinous malpractice lawsuits forces doctors to practice "defensive medicine"—ordering numerous costly tests and procedures that are unlikely to benefit the patient, just to make sure the doctor doesn't miss something and hence be exposed to malpractice liability. The need to practice defensive medicine significantly drives up the cost of health care.

There are various proposals that could control this aspect of medical costs. They fall under the label of "tort reform"—"tort" meaning a wrong, including medical malpractice, for which the victim can seek monetary compensation in a civil lawsuit. The idea of tort reform is to find a better balance between the right of victims to be compensated for their injuries and the need of society as a whole to contain soaring health care costs. Common tort reform proposals include putting limits on the amount that juries can award in punitive damages and for pain and suffering; and discouraging frivolous lawsuits by requiring the loser in any lawsuit to pay the winner's attorney's fees. Another reform is to eliminate or modify "joint and several liability," the traditional rule that can force a doctor to pay 100 percent of a malpractice victim's damages even if the doctor was only partially responsible for the victim's injuries.

Tort reform, like interstate competition in health insurance, is important to controlling costs, but to return to the main point: The real key to making health care affordable is empowering patients to act as consumers in a competitive market. When health care becomes patient-centered—rather than bureaucrat-centered or insurance company-centered—we will be well on the way to building a system that works for all of us.

An important issue remains, however: How do we help people who are difficult to insure because of pre-existing conditions? James Capretta and Tom Miller, two of the authors of *Why Obamacare is Wrong for America*, propose establishing high-risk pools to serve such people. Insurance companies would be given incentives to participate in these pools, and individuals purchasing insurance through them would be subsidized as necessary. Capretta and Miller acknowledge that these high-risk pools will require significant taxpayer support, but that this would pale in comparison to the massive costs of Obamacare.[108]

I won't go into the details of Capretta and Miller's proposal (which differs greatly from temporary high-risk pools established under Obamacare), but will suggest some general principles: If we're going to establish new entitlements, we need to focus on the people who really need help. That seems obvious, but that concept seems to have been lost on the Politicrats who designed Obamacare. Prior to the passage of Obamacare, 89 percent of Americans were satisfied with their health care.[109] Obamacare sought to fix problems that affect a minority of the population through a massive bureaucratic intrusion that would be disruptive, expensive and harmful to the 89 percent that were happy as they were. It was a classic case of throwing the baby out with the bathwater, and of dragging people kicking and screaming into a Brave New World that they didn't ask for.

If we need to spend money to help people who can't afford insurance because they're poor, or because they're priced out of the market because of pre-existing conditions, then let's find a way to do it. Let's keep in mind, though, that in an era where the federal government has to borrow 40 cents out of every dollar that it spends, instituting a new open-ended entitlement program is like writing a check drawn on your toddler's savings account. That doesn't mean that we don't try to take care of people who really need it now; it means that we focus our spending wisely so that we can afford to help those people.

We can reform our health care system so that it works for the most vulnerable in our society—and for everyone else as well. To do so, we need more competition rather than more government control. Our health care system should march not to the tune of the insurance companies, the bureaucrats, the trial lawyers, the lobbyists, or the other moneyed special interests, but to the tune of the average folks who are just trying to get well and stay well. Power to the Patients!

8 A NATION OF IMMIGRANTS

Anyone who thinks we abolished slavery in America in the 1860s should read the excellent book *Nobodies* by investigative journalist John Bowe.[110] Bowe takes us to hidden immigrant labor compounds that few Americans would believe could possibly exist in our country in this day and age.

The book opens as a real-life murder mystery, set in the swamplands of rural Florida. A Guatemalan migrant has been discovered dead, face down in a pool of blood. He was a *chofer*, a van driver whose job was to transport the farm hands to and from the fields. According to anonymous witnesses, the driver had been pulled out of his van by several men and shot execution-style. The shooting took place in a "migrant-worker ghetto," which Bowe describes as "a mishmash of rotting trailer homes and plywood shacks" that are "hidden outside the town of Lake Placid, a mile or two back from the main road."

The residents of the isolated shanty town are illegal immigrants from Mexico and Central America. Bowe sets the context by describing the plight of migrant workers in general: "Since they frequently come with little money and few connections, the contractor, or crew boss, as he's often called, often provides food, housing, and transportation to and from work. As a result, many farmworkers labor under the near-total control of their employers." This particular migrant camp houses hundreds of crop pickers in the employ of a contractor named Ramiro Ramos, whom the workers have nicknamed "El Diablo."

The sheriff's deputies' investigation brings them into a hidden world within their midst that they had previously known little about:

> With each new detail, an increasingly disturbing picture of Ramos's operation began to emerge. El Diablo, it seemed, had been lending money to his workers, then overcharging them for substandard "barracks-style" housing, gouging them with miscellaneous fees, and encouraging them to shop at a high-priced grocery store, conveniently owned by his wife. By the time El Diablo had deducted for this, that, and the other thing, workers said, they were barely breaking even.

> Worse, they were trapped. El Diablo's labor camp was in a tiny, isolated country town. He and his family, a network of cousins and in-laws, many of whom also worked as labor contractors, patrolled the area in their massive Ford F-250 pickup trucks, communicating with one another through Nextel walkie-talkie phones. For foreigners unfamiliar with the area, escape was almost unthinkable. But just to make matters crystal clear, El Diablo told his workers that anyone indebted caught trying to run away would be killed.

> The previous night's murder, the witnesses alleged, had taken place when an indebted employee had left. The murder was meant to send a signal to local workers and to *chofers* thinking about aiding their departure from El Diablo's territory.

If the case sounds like a slam dunk, what happened next was, unfortunately, all too common in cases involving undocumented workers. After spilling most of the beans off the record, all the informants but one declined to name Ramos or his accomplices as the perpetrators, or even to offer their own names. One of the passengers in the murder victim's van told detectives that he couldn't remember a single thing about the incident....

Another witness acknowledged seeing the murder but, according to the sheriff's report, refused to name the shooter, stating his belief that "if he told, he would be killed by the Ramos family." The Ramoses knew where his family lived in Mexico, he said; if they didn't kill him personally, they would kill one of his relatives.

I won't tell you the rest of the story. If you want to see how it turns out, buy the book—which also details the incredibly arduous labor these migrants perform for pay that most teenage baby sitters would find insulting. Later in the book, Bowe recounts how a U.S. Border Patrol agent summarized the predicament workers like these find themselves in:

"You know," he said, "these workers are so vulnerable. They're housed miles from civilization, with no telephones or cars. Whatever they're told they're gonna do, they're gonna do. They're controllable. There's no escape. If you do escape, what are you gonna do? Run seventeen miles to the nearest town? When you don't even know where it is? And, if you have a brother or a cousin in the group, are you gonna leave them behind? You gonna escape with seventeen people? You're gonna make

tracks like a herd of elephants. They'll find you.
And heaven help you when they do."

How is this not slavery? And more importantly, how can this
type of thing be allowed to go on in modern-day America?

John Bowe's politics are much closer to Liberal Dave's than
ConservaDave's, but ConservaDave was quite moved by *Nobodies*.
Both Liberal Dave and ConservaDave (whom we can collectively
refer to as the "Daves"), like almost all Americans, are of immigrant
stock. The Daves's "only in America" mongrel lineage stands out
for its incongruity, even in this nation of immigrants: "Jewish-
Samoan" almost sounds like the punch line of a joke. The life that
some of the Daves's ancestors escaped was no laughing matter,
however. Their maternal grandfather, the son of a laborer, was born
and raised in a small Jewish village in Grajewo (pronounced Grah-
yeh-vah), part of the territory that Russia and Poland traded back and
forth over the years. The Jews of Grajewo were slaughtered en
masse by the Poles and Nazis in July 1941.[111]   By that time,
however, the family was safely in New York. The Daves's maternal
grandmother was the daughter of a tailor from a Russian *shtel*—a
small Jewish village of the type featured in *Fiddler on the Roof*.

On the other end of the world, the Daves's paternal grandfather
was a minister from the village of Salani on the island of Upolu,
Samoa. Their paternal grandmother, who hailed from the village of
Sapapali'i on the island of Savai'i, Samoa, descended from a line of
Samoan *Malietoa*—the dynastic chiefly title that had been bestowed
on Samoa's rulers for hundreds of years. The oddness of the
Daves's Samoan and Jewish combination is perhaps even trumped
by their lineal melding of peasantry and royalty. Only in America
indeed.

Samoa, then known as "Western Samoa," was a protectorate of
New Zealand at the time. But the Daves's paternal grandparents
somehow found their way—"immigrated," if you will—into

neighboring American Samoa, the U.S. territory where the Daves's father was born.

Because of their background, both Liberal Dave and ConservaDave have always identified with immigrants.

Immigration, like many issues, divides liberals and conservatives. At the risk of over-generalizing, liberals seem to have more sympathy for the plight of illegal aliens than do conservatives. In fact, many liberals find the term "illegal alien" offensive because it's stigmatizing; they instead use the nonjudgmental term "undocumented workers."

Conservatives, on the other hand, bridle at the use of such euphemisms. Why, conservatives ask, do some people want to obfuscate the fact that illegal immigration is indeed illegal, and an affront to our national sovereignty? Is the rejection of the term "illegal" intended to suggest that Americans do not have the right to determine, through their democratically elected representatives, the rules governing entry into their own country? That the will of the American people need not be respected?

Many liberals support "sanctuary city" programs, where certain cities forbid their police and other city employees from asking anyone about their immigration status and refuse to allow local resources to be used to enforce federal immigration law. Proponents argue that sanctuary city policies protect the health and safety not only of illegal immigrants, but of the entire community. When witnesses to crime are afraid to come forward for fear of being deported, for example, it makes the police's job harder. Similarly, it makes it harder for public health officials to control the spread of disease if a certain portion of the community is intent on hiding from the authorities.

Conservatives, on the other hand, tend to abhor sanctuary cities as an affront to the rule of law. Conservatives suspect liberal urban politicians of simply ignoring immigration laws because they don't believe in enforcing them. Conservatives believe that sanctuary city policies lead to a dangerous mixing of messages to illegal immigrants that encourages more of them to come here: "No matter what the federal law says, you're welcome here."

There has been a backlash against sanctuary cities, reflected in laws that are designed to tell illegal aliens that they are not, in fact, welcome here. In 2010, the City of Costa Mesa, California, declared itself a "Rule of Law" community that will uphold immigration laws.[112]

More importantly, though, a number of states have passed tough laws designed to encourage illegal aliens to go elsewhere. Arizona started the trend in 2010, enacting an immigration law that triggered massive protests throughout the country.[113]

One of the most controversial provisions of the Arizona law is a requirement that police officers determine the immigration status of a person whom they stop, detain or arrest if there is "reasonable suspicion" that the person is an illegal immigrant. This is often referred to as the "show me your papers" requirement. Civil rights activists have denounced this provision as racist, contending that reasonable suspicion of illegal status would almost certainly be based upon a person's Latino appearance.[114]

President Obama criticized the law shortly after it was passed. "You can imagine if you are a Hispanic American in Arizona, your great grandparents may have been there before Arizona was even a state," he said. "Now suddenly if you don't have your papers and you take your kid out for ice cream and you're going to be harassed, that's not the right way to go."[115]

The law, however, does not allow a police officer to harass someone who was simply taking his kid out for ice cream. A police officer is only authorized to request proof of status from someone who has been lawfully stopped, detained or arrested for something unrelated to immigration. The law does not authorize a person to be stopped for "breathing while brown," as some have suggested;[116] there must be a separate legitimate basis—at least a traffic violation—to stop, detain or arrest the person. And the police are only required to inquire into someone's immigration status if there is "reasonable suspicion" that the person is an illegal alien—and the law specifically prohibits that suspicion to be based upon racial profiling. If a person who is asked by the police about his immigration status can produce so much as a valid driver's license, the inquiry can go no further.[117]

Those who call the law "racist" are not impressed with the law's express prohibition against racial profiling. As a practical matter, they say, the police will engage in racial profiling even if the law says they can't; people with an ethnic Mexican appearance will be asked for their papers, and those who look Anglo will not. But consider this comparison with federal law: If a federal immigration agent wants to ask someone for his immigration papers, he doesn't have to jump through the hurdles that are imposed upon an Arizona police officer: there doesn't have to be a lawful stop, detention or arrest on an unrelated matter, there doesn't have to be "reasonable suspicion" that the person is an illegal alien, and there is no express prohibition against racial profiling. How, then, could one call the Arizona law racist without concluding that federal immigration law is even more racist?

It is noteworthy that when Attorney General Eric Holder filed the Obama Administration's lawsuit against Arizona over its immigration law, he did not include a claim that the law was discriminatory or violated anyone's civil rights.[118] Given how the President and others in his administration had criticized the law on the grounds that it would promote discrimination, the Attorney General presumably would have included a civil rights claim in the lawsuit had there been a valid one. Instead, the lawsuit claimed that Arizona's attempt to enforce immigration law would get in the way of the federal government's efforts to enforce immigration law. The irony here is that the federal government has sued Arizona over a law designed to *assist* in the enforcement of federal immigration law, but the feds have failed to take action against sanctuary city laws that actively *thwart* the enforcement of federal immigration law.

The Obama Administration's lawsuit, by the way, was partially successful: The Supreme Court struck down some provisions of the Arizona law, but upheld the controversial "show me your papers" requirement.

Since Arizona passed its law, other states have followed suit with immigration laws that are as tough or even tougher.[119] Liberals typically denounce these laws and their supporters for scapegoating immigrants. Conservatives chafe at the "anti-immigrant" label; they claim that it is only *illegal* immigration that they oppose, and denounce liberals for disingenuously blurring the distinction between legal and illegal immigration.

One conservative proposal that raises hackles from the left is the idea of building a fence across the entire 1952-mile long U.S. border with Mexico.[120] Liberal columnist Jorge Castaneda expressed his objections as follows: "[I]t's a terrible message to send to both societies that the United States wants to build a wall or is building a wall to try and keep people out or, for that matter, to keep things in, like guns or money or chemicals. It's a lousy idea, it sends the wrong message. This is not the type of symbol that you want erected on the border between two countries that seek to be closer and closer friends and allies and partners over the years."[121]

Conservative columnist Charles Krauthammer, though, believes that many bogus arguments have been tossed around in what he calls the "ridiculous debate over the building of a fence":

> Despite the success of the border barrier in the San Diego area, it appears to be very important that this success not be repeated. The current Senate bill[122] provides for the fencing of no more than one-fifth of the border and the placing of vehicle barriers in no more than one-ninth.

Instead, we are promised all kinds of fancy, high-tech substitutes—sensors, cameras, unmanned aerial vehicles—and lots more armed chaps on the ground to go chasing those who get through.

Why? A barrier is a very simple thing to do. The technology is well tested. The Chinese had success with it, as did Hadrian. In our time, the barrier Israel has built has been so effective in keeping out intruders that suicide attacks are down over 90 percent.

Fences work. That's why people have them around their houses—not because homeowners are unwelcoming, but because they insist that those who wish to come into their domain knock at the front door.

Fences are simple. They don't require much upkeep. Two fences with a patrol road between them across the length of the U.S.-Mexico border would be relatively cheap, easy to build and simple to maintain.

Why this preference for the fancy high-tech surveillance stuff that presents no physical impediment to illegal entry but instead triggers detection—followed by alarm, pursuit, arrest and possible violence? It makes for great TV. But why is that good for the country?

It is certainly good for the Border Patrol, ensuring a full employment program till the end of time. But why for the rest of us? Fences have no retirement benefits.

The final argument against fences is, of course, the symbolism. We don't want a fence that announces to the world that America is closed. But this is entirely irrational. The fact is that under our law, America is indeed closed—to all but those who, after elaborate procedures, are deemed worthy of joining the American family. Those objecting to the fence should be objecting to the law that closes America off, not to the means for effectively carrying out that law.

A fence announces to the world that America is closed to ... illegal immigrants. What's wrong with that? Is not every country in the world the same? The only reason others don't need such a barrier is because they are not half as attractive as America, not because we are more oppressive or less welcoming.

Fences are ugly, I grant you that. But not as ugly as 12 million people living in the shadows in a country that has forfeited control of its borders.[123]

After devoting an entire column to refuting liberal arguments against a border fence, Krauthammer saves a tantalizing concession to liberals for last: "Once our borders come visibly under control, everything else will become doable. Including amnesty."

Wow, he actually said the "A" word (or wrote it, I should say). If Social Security is the "third rail" of American politics, then amnesty is the third rail of conservative politics. Conservatives are generally galled at the thought of people being rewarded for breaking the law. Even most conservatives, though, recognize that it would be impractical and prohibitively expensive to round up and deport 12 million or more illegal aliens.

At the other end of the spectrum, though, it is also impractical and indeed dangerous to continue to tolerate a situation where our border can be crossed illegally with impunity. Some immigration rights advocates have a reflexive aversion to tough border security; they fret about the "militarization of the border" and waging "war on undocumented immigrants."[124]   These advocates assert that the people who cross our southern border are doing so to provide for their families, and pose no threat to our national security. That is mostly true. But if impoverished laborers can sneak over our border almost at will, then how could we expect that well-financed terrorist organizations, drug cartels, spy rings and other dangerous groups would have any trouble sneaking their people in as well? In the age of terrorism, our porous border has become a liability that is simply intolerable. Some point out that securing our border will not solve the illegal immigration problem, since a large percentage of illegal aliens do not sneak across the border; they enter legally and overstay their visas. Fine, we have to work on that as well, but that's hardly a justification for leaving ourselves dangerously exposed with an improperly secured border.

It would be wrong, however, to say that securing the border is solely a national security imperative that we must pursue at the expense of illegal immigrants. Securing the border is also a moral imperative that we should pursue in order to protect the illegal immigrants themselves—as well as those who might be tempted to sneak across the border in the future. The U.S.-Mexico border, almost 2,000 miles long, is the world's longest international border between a rich nation and a poor nation.   That guarantees a continuous flow of migrants northward unless and until the border is properly secured. As long as people have the temptation and the ability to sneak into our country to work illegally, we will continue to have the hidden slave camps described in John Bowe's book.

It may sound provocative to suggest that lax border security leads to modern-day slavery, but it is clearly true. Illegal aliens are the most exploitable people in our society. Their lack of status makes them so desperate to avoid the authorities that they will allow unscrupulous employers to get away with anything—cheating, beating, imprisonment, and worse. As long as we have a continuous supply of workers living in the shadows, we will have people willing to subject them to the most horrific oppression in order to profit from their cheap labor.

We could, of course, bring illegal aliens out of the shadows by offering them amnesty. Without a secure border, though, that type of policy becomes self-defeating. Granting amnesty to illegal aliens who are already here only encourages more to sneak over the border. The new arrivals will then become the new hidden underclass, hoping that it will one day be their turn to get amnesty. We tried granting amnesty to illegal aliens during the Reagan Administration, as part of a comprehensive solution that would also secure the border and crack down on employers who hired illegal aliens. Unfortunately, we never built a border fence, and did not devote sufficient resources to securing the border or prosecuting employers. The amnesty—the one part of the comprehensive solution that really did materialize—led to a sharp upsurge in illegal immigration. The "comprehensive solution" succeeded only in making the problem much worse.[125]

The lesson from the failed 1980s effort is clear: the border must be secured *before* legal status is offered to illegal aliens. Otherwise, we'll just be encouraging more illegal immigration without the ability to stop it. And until we build a proper barrier across the entire border, our vague promises to secure the border will neither be credible nor effective.

Building a barrier—and hence getting *real* control over the border—will not, as some have claimed, be a symbol of our inhumanity to our neighbors. To the contrary, it would free us to be humane. We could be humane to illegal aliens who are already here by offering them a pathway to legalization and eventual citizenship, secure in the knowledge that our generosity would not be punished by a new and larger flood of illegal immigration. We could be humane to our impoverished neighbors in Mexico and Central America, crafting reasonable policies that align our need for labor with their need for economic opportunity. Crafting these policies would be an exercise of our popular will and the right that every sovereign nation has to decide who may and may not enter—in contrast to the disregard of our sovereignty that is inherent in illegal immigration.

Detractors argue that no barrier will prevent people from sneaking into the country. That may be true, but experience and common sense tell us that a properly designed barrier can greatly reduce unauthorized border crossings. An imperfect barrier that allows a trickle of illegal immigration is greatly preferable to a mostly barrier-less boundary that allows a flood.

A secure border would of course have to be complemented by strong interior enforcement. We need to expand the use of E-Verify, the Department of Homeland Security's online system that allows employers to verify the immigration status of employees and prospective employees. And we need to be much tougher on employers who knowingly hire illegal aliens. Most conservatives resist efforts to de-stigmatize illegal aliens with euphemisms such as "undocumented workers"—but we should recognize that the employers who hire them should be stigmatized much more than the workers. Who, after all, is more worthy of scorn: a worker trying to escape grinding poverty in order to feed his family, or an employer who is eager to exploit that worker's desperate situation in order to make a buck? The worst-offending employers, of course, are beyond shame, and hence should be "stigmatized" where they'll feel it—in their wallets.

Once our border is largely under control, we can bring the millions of illegal aliens in our midst out of hiding. They will be much harder to exploit in the sunlight than in the shadows; there will be fewer hidden atrocities occurring under the American flag.

We can eventually invite our newly legalized workers to become full members of the American family. But before we do so, we need to take care of some unfinished business. By entering the country illegally, these aliens "jumped in line" ahead of millions of people from around the world who have sought to enter our country the right way. Some have been waiting patiently for years. These legal applicants have respected our sovereignty and our right to control our own borders. It is only right that we return that respect, and not reward those who have disregarded our laws with an unfair advantage over those who have followed them. If we ever pass legislation granting illegal aliens a pathway to citizenship, we should at the very least make sure that the backlog of legal immigration applications is processed before we grant permanent status to those who entered the country illegally.

Many liberal activists have worked hard to protect illegal aliens from exploitation. But they will always be fighting a losing battle until we adopt a policy favored by conservatives: a good fence will indeed make good neighbors, and will allow us to improve the lives of workers on both sides of the border.

9 ENVIRONMENTALISM: SEPARATING CHURCH FROM STATE

If environmentalism were a religion, then Van Jones would be its most charismatic preacher. A compelling speaker, Jones sells a vision where the greening of our economy will be our path to economic prosperity. We don't have to choose between the competing goals of creating jobs and protecting the environment— that's the old way of thinking, fed to us by the dinosaur industrialists of the "pollution-based economy." We can have our cake and eat it too, if only we change the way we think.

Jones laid out his vision for a green future—both environmentally and financially—in a 2007 speech in San Francisco:

> We know, that when you come up with the technologies, and when the President signs the laws to make it right, that that President—whoever he, or she, is—is not gonna put up one solar panel. The President is not gonna weatherize one building. But we're gonna have to weatherize millions and millions of buildings so they don't leak so much energy. We've got to put up millions of solar panels. That's millions of jobs.

We say, "Give the people that most need the work the opportunity to do the work that most needs to be done." Take these young people in the neighborhood who are going to funerals every other weekend. They're going to schools, classrooms, 36 kids in the classroom, six books, no chalk, no toilet paper—these young people who've been thrown away, let's go to them! And say to them:

"We need you! We have a place for you. We want to put the tools and the training and the technology in your hands." We have to retrofit a nation. We have to reboot and retrofit a nation. We want you to put those solar panels up on your gramamma's house. We want you to be the one that brings her energy bill down. Because when YOU learn how to put up solar panels, you're on your way to becoming, sister, an electrical engineer. You can join a union as a green pathway out of poverty. If you want to weatherize a building, when you double pane that glass, you're on your way to becoming a glazer. You can join a union, that's a green pathway out of poverty. And the good thing about it is we gotta get you in on the ground floor, it's a growing industry. You might start off right now putting up the solar panels but in two years, they're gonna hire some people under you and you can become a manager. You can help other people do this. You can become your own business person someday.

You see, that's what this green economy is all about. It's gonna be able to give us the opportunity to rebuild and reinvest in America, and guess who gets to benefit the most? The people who have been the most locked down and left out of the pollution-based economy. Those are the ones who get to be locked in now, to the clean and green economy.

And so, when we bring these movements together— the best of the business community, the best of the technology community, and the best of our racial justice, anti-poverty forces—and we stand shoulder to shoulder, we get the coalition that we've always wanted.[126]

Van Jones connected the dots in ways that others hadn't. Environmentalism wasn't a chic indulgence that only the affluent could afford. It had the potential to reach into the inner city and lift people out of poverty.

Jones's star would rise after President Obama took office in 2009. He was appointed as a "green jobs" advisor to the White House Council on Environmental Quality in March 2009. His tenure in the Obama Administration was short, however. He resigned in September 2009 after various controversies came to light. For example, Jones signed a petition suggesting the Bush Administration may have purposely allowed the 9/11 attacks to happen as a pretext for war.[127] Also, in a speaking engagement the month before he joined the White House, he referred to Republicans as "a**holes."[128]

In March 2009, the same month that Van Jones joined the White House staff, Obama's Energy Department announced that a $535 million loan guarantee would be granted to California solar panel manufacturer Solyndra Inc. Jones had nothing to do with that loan guarantee, which had been in the works long before he arrived in Washington, but Solyndra symbolized the green energy future that Jones had spoken so passionately about. The company had been hand-picked to receive the first loan guarantee for an energy project under Obama's economic stimulus program. Solyndra represented the promise of green technology: Environmentalism that doesn't cost jobs, but creates jobs.

The Obama Administration was so anxious to announce the Solyndra loan guarantee—the first major accomplishment of its green energy program—that it significantly sped up its approval process. Energy Secretary Steven Chu, in a press release announcing the transaction, took pride in how quickly his department was able to complete its review: "Secretary Chu initially set a target to have the first conditional commitments out by May— three months into his tenure—but today's announcement significantly outpaces that aggressive timeline. Secretary Chu credited the Department's loan team for their work accelerating the process to offer this conditional commitment in less than two months."[129]

Solyndra broke ground on a state-of-the-art new factory in September 2009. Secretary Chu was there to wield one of the ceremonial groundbreaking shovels, and Vice President Biden was patched in by teleconference. "This announcement today is part of the unprecedented investment this Administration is making in renewable energy and exactly what the Recovery Act is all about," said the Vice President. Everyone was filled with sunny optimism, but clouds would soon appear on the horizon.

Six months later, PricewaterhouseCoopers issued an audit of Solyndra that came to a troubling conclusion: "The Company has suffered recurring losses from operations, negative cash flows since inception and has a net stockholders' deficit that, among other factors, raise substantial doubt about its ability to continue as a going concern."

Undaunted, President Obama paid a visit to the Solyndra plant in May 2010, two months after the PricewaterhouseCoopers audit had been issued. "The true engine of economic growth will always be companies like Solyndra," said the President.

On November 3, 2010, Solyndra announced that it would shut down one of its factories and lay off 40 workers and 150 contractors. The announcement was made one day after the Congressional mid-term elections. It turns out that the timing was no coincidence: according to emails that would later be released, the Energy Department "push[ed] very hard" for Solyndra to delay its announcement, originally planned for October, until November 3.[130]

On August 31, 2011, Solyndra ceased operations, causing over 1,100 employees to lose their jobs. The company filed for bankruptcy less than a week later, on September 6, 2011. The FBI raided the company's corporate headquarters two days after that, carrying out boxes full of documents.

In the wake of the Solyndra bankruptcy, information started to come out suggesting that the Obama Administration had ignored warning signals as it rushed through its approval process. Solyndra had applied for the loan guarantee during the Bush Administration but shortly before the Bush team left office, the Energy Department's credit committee decided against moving forward with the project.[131] The Obama team, however, put the project back on track—the fast track—soon after it arrived. Subsequently released emails show direct pressure from the White House to rush a decision on the loan. An Office of Management and Budget official wrote in a March 2009 email that the Solyndra deal "is NOT ready for prime time." Ten days later, however, the deal was announced.

It also came to light that major Obama campaign donor George Kaiser, whose family foundation was Solyndra's biggest investor, was a very frequent visitor to the White House in the early days of the Obama Administration. Emails suggested that he discussed the Solyndra deal with top White House officials.[132] Kaiser, a billionaire, led an investment group that provided a $75 million loan to Solyndra in February 2011. As part of that deal, the U.S. government took the unusual step of agreeing to subordinate itself to Kaiser's group in the event Solyndra went bankrupt. In other words, the $75 million would have to be repaid to Kaiser's group before taxpayers could get most of their money back. If the bankruptcy process couldn't salvage enough money to pay Kaiser's group the full $75 million, then the taxpayers would be out of luck.[133]

Other suggestions of political influence began to surface. Emails revealed that another major Obama fundraiser who was hired to help oversee the energy loan program put constant pressure on Energy Department officials to quickly decide on Solyndra's application. His wife's law firm was representing Solyndra at the time. Indeed, several top Obama campaign contributors had ended up working in the Energy Department as it doled out billions of stimulus dollars to alternative energy companies.

The Solyndra affair at the very least creates the appearance of the crony capitalism that the Occupy Wall Street protestors claimed to be so exorcised about. The "green" that came out of Solyndra was primarily the hundreds of millions of taxpayer greenbacks excreted into the environmentally friendly low-flush toilet. And while ConservaDave would hate to say "I told you so," Solyndra clearly demonstrates the dangers of allowing Politicrats to pick winners and losers by showering billions and billions of taxpayer dollars on favored companies. It undermines the public's trust in government when Politicrats award benefits to well-connected donors, even in cases where no law-breaking is officially proven. When government gets involved, clean technology begets unclean politics. And Politicrats make lousy venture capitalists—because of ineptitude, the corrupting influence of politics, or both. Like comedy, venture capitalism should be left to the professionals.

This is not to say that green technology does not hold tremendous promise to make our lives better in the future. The problem lies in thinking that the government can somehow create sustainable jobs out of technologies that have not yet proven their viability in the marketplace. It is the marketplace that will ultimately have to pick the winners and losers, and government needs to have more humility about its ability to move the process along.

Therein lies the fatal flaw of Van Jones's vision. His concept of a green future, where "green collar jobs" will provide the ladder of opportunity for those who need it the most, is almost entirely government-driven. That is not surprising, because Mr. Jones is not an entrepreneur. He is not a venture capitalist. He is not a scientist. He is an activist, and he thinks and speaks like an activist. Activism doesn't create jobs, though—at least not sustainable jobs in the real world. Listen to his language: "millions of jobs" will be created not when entrepreneurs and financiers do their thing, but "when the President signs the laws to make it right." In Jones's activist view of the world, jobs are created through political coalition-building: "And so, when we bring these movements together—the best of the business community, the best of the technology community, and the best of our racial justice, anti-poverty forces—and we stand shoulder to shoulder, we get the coalition that we've always wanted."

It is this type of political model for job creation that brought us Solyndra. Jones became popular because he articulated a thesis that liberals very much wanted to hear: The purported choice between protecting the environment and creating economic opportunities for the poor is a false choice. We can have it all—a clean environment at absolutely no cost in terms of jobs. That's a seductive message for us all, but particularly for liberals: having to choose between jobs and the environment creates significant tensions among factions that make up the modern liberal coalition—tensions between environmentalists and the unions, between environmentalists and advocates for the poor. By conjuring a future where these tensions will no longer exist, Jones professes the ability to bring harmony to "the coalition we always wanted."

The Great Green Future—where clean technologies can generate sustainable jobs and prosperity on a large scale—may well come about. We should all hope that it does. But it is beyond the capabilities of government to will that future into existence—unless we're willing to tolerate an astounding amount of wasted money and corruption along the way.

Alas, that Great Green Future has yet to arrive, and so the tradeoff between environmental protection and our economic well-being is alive and well. From a 2010 Heritage Foundation report:

> The policies to cap carbon dioxide and mandate "clean" energy production are very expensive. The cap and trade bill passed by the House of Representatives would result in 1.9 million fewer jobs in 2012, $9.4 trillion in lost economic growth from 2012–2035, and a 90% increase in the price of electricity by 2035. Proposals for a renewable electricity mandate, which would require 20% of our nation's electricity (currently at 3%) to come from government-picked renewable sources, are not much better. They would destroy over one million jobs (on net), cut national income (GDP) by $5.2 trillion between 2012 and 2035, and increase electricity prices 36%. Neither policy would have any noticeable environmental impact, but both would result in more government control of the economy and thus more lobbyists flooding the halls of Congress to pursue their special interests.[134]

If the choice between aggressive environmental protection and our economic health is really a "false choice," don't tell that to Senator Joe Manchin (D-West Virginia). He won election to the Senate in 2010, a very difficult year for his fellow Democrats. He campaigned on his strong opposition to the Obama-supported cap and trade bill, the draconian economic impacts of which were estimated above by the Heritage Foundation. (The bill would cap the amount of certain pollutants that each business could discharge, but allow businesses to trade their discharge allotments with other businesses.) In his most famous ad, Manchin promised to take "dead aim" at the cap and trade bill—and then took his rifle and shot a hole through a copy of the bill, which was helplessly pinned to a tree.[135] He also bragged in his ad about having sued the Environmental Protection Agency, which many Republicans blame for killing jobs with excessive regulation.[136]

The recent controversy over the $7 billion Keystone XL pipeline project also highlights the tradeoff between environmental protection and economic prosperity. An article in *Mother Jones* describes a 2011 public meeting on the project as "an unusual scene, a packed room of environmentalists and union members who were, in an unusual twist, mostly on opposite sides of the dispute. Several hundred union members showed up in bright orange and lime green T-shirts, in a show of support for the proposed 1,661-mile pipeline from Canada to Texas. Environmentalists were also out in force to urge the State Department to stop Transcanada, a Canadian energy company, from moving forward with the project."

A member of the Laborers' International Union of North America explained why he came out to support a project that environmentalists so staunchly opposed: "People are struggling for jobs," he said. "You have to survive, pay our bills and things like that."[137]

The Keystone XL pipeline project illustrates not only the tradeoff between environmental protection and jobs, but also between environmental protection and our pursuit of energy independence. The pipeline would bring 700,000 barrels of oil per day into the U.S.[138] That is oil that we would not have to purchase from hostile countries like Venezuela, or countries like Saudi Arabia that use their oil profits to fund the spread of religious fanaticism.

Of course, renewable energy will hopefully make us energy independent in the future. That is the environmentalists' dream, and it is a dream we should all share. But if we believe that aggressive government mandates can make us energy independent without ruining our economy, then we are truly dreaming. As the Heritage study suggests, aggressive government mandates are not a path to an energy independent future, but rather a path to hell paved with good intentions.

The Keystone XL debate also suggests that the environmental movement has fallen prey to a troubling absolutism. As reported in *The New York Times*, the Obama Administration's own environmental impact assessment of the proposed pipeline found that it would pose few environmental risks.[139] Kenneth Green, a Resident Scholar at the American Enterprise Institute, dismissed the concerns raised by environmental groups. Noting that China would buy Canada's oil if we didn't, Green wrote:

> [W]hether the U.S. buys it or Canada ships it to China or other countries, the oil will be extracted, transported, refined and burned. And whether it's greenhouse gases you're concerned about, particulate matter or any other sort of pollution related to oil production and consumption, they're going to enter the atmosphere whether they do so here or elsewhere. In fact, given North America's extremely tight environmental standards, the impact of producing, transporting and refining Canada's oil would probably be *less* here than elsewhere. As for the local risks to aquifers and the like, existing analyses show low risks from the Keystone XL, even to fragile ecosystems that it may traverse — certainly far less risk than moving oil across that same region by truck or train. And considering that far more oil enters the environment from tanker accidents than from pipelines, importing oil from the Middle East is probably worse for the environment than importing it from Canada through the Keystone pipeline would

be.[140]

Some would say that the modern environmental movement reflexively opposes major projects, and finds it distasteful to subject environmental policies to the same type of cost-benefit analysis that is routinely applied to other policies. "How can you put a price tag on clean air, clean water, our own health, and the health of our children?" environmentalists often ask. That's a good question. But how too can you put a price tag on people losing their ability to support their families, of having their health impaired, their life spans shortened, because we pursued policies without regard for their economic and fiscal impacts? How can you put a price tag on the lives that have been taken by the violent extremism funded by the money we send overseas—because we refuse to tap our own energy resources? As gauche as it may seem, there are many things that we "can't put a price tag on" that we indeed must put a price tag on, recognizing, as adults, that our important policy choices will inevitably have serious impacts in both directions. We rarely get the luxury of policy choices between "all good" and "all bad," which is why we have to honestly evaluate the costs and benefits of competing alternatives.

This chapter opened with the words "[i]f environmentalism were a religion...." The late science fiction author Michael Crichton believed that environmentalism had essentially become just that. In a famous speech before the Commonwealth Club of San Francisco in 2003, Crichton called environmentalism "one of the most powerful religions in the Western World," and indeed "the religion of choice for urban atheists." He was not paying environmentalism a compliment. "Increasingly it seems facts aren't necessary, because the tenets of environmentalism are all about belief," said the author. "It's about whether you are going to be a sinner, or saved. Whether you are going to be one of the people on the side of salvation, or on the side of doom. Whether you are going to be one of us, or one of them."[141]

Crichton went on to rattle off a number of things that the claimed the environmental movement had gotten wrong, sometimes causing great human suffering:

> I know you haven't read any of what I am about to tell you in the newspaper, because newspapers literally don't report them. I can tell you that [the pesticide] DDT is not a carcinogen and did not cause birds to die and should never have been banned. I can tell you that the people who banned it knew that it wasn't carcinogenic and banned it anyway. I can tell you that the DDT ban has caused the deaths of tens of millions of poor people, mostly children, whose deaths are directly attributable to a callous, technologically advanced western society that promoted the new cause of environmentalism by pushing a fantasy about a pesticide, and thus irrevocably harmed the third world. Banning DDT is one of the most disgraceful episodes in the twentieth century history of America. We knew better, and we did it anyway, and we let people around the world die and didn't give a damn.
>
> I can tell you that second hand smoke is not a health hazard to anyone and never was, and the EPA has always known it. I can tell you that the evidence for global warming is far weaker than its proponents would ever admit. I can tell you the percentage of the US land area that is taken by urbanization, including cities and roads, is 5%. I can tell you that the Sahara desert is shrinking, and the total ice of Antarctica is increasing. I can tell you that a blue-ribbon panel in Science magazine concluded that there is no known

technology that will enable us to halt the rise of carbon dioxide in the 21st century. Not wind, not solar, not even nuclear. The panel concluded a totally new technology—like nuclear fusion—was necessary, otherwise nothing could be done and in the meantime all efforts would be a waste of time. They said that when the UN IPCC reports stated alternative technologies existed that could control greenhouse gases, the UN was wrong.

It is possible that reasonable people could debate some of Crichton's statements, perhaps with evidence that has come to light since 2003. These debates should evolve over time as evidence comes and goes. But Crichton's complaint was that environmentalism's "religious" mindset has stifled the debate:

Religions think they know it all, but the unhappy truth of the environment is that we are dealing with incredibly complex, evolving systems, and we usually are not certain how best to proceed. Those who are certain are demonstrating their personality type, or their belief system, not the state of their knowledge. Our record in the past, for example managing national parks, is humiliating. Our fifty-year effort at forest-fire suppression is a well-intentioned disaster from which our forests will never recover. We need to be humble, deeply humble, in the face of what we are trying to accomplish. We need to be trying various methods of accomplishing things. We need to be open-minded about assessing results of our efforts, and we need to be flexible about balancing needs. Religions are good at none of these things.

The religious fervor that has seized environmental activism has fostered an aversion to acknowledging tradeoffs. We have discussed the tradeoffs between environmentalism and the economy, between environmentalism and energy independence. But ironically, environmentalists are sometimes oblivious even to tradeoffs between environmentalism and environmentalism, failing to think through the net environmental harm that can result from supposedly eco-friendly policies.

Columnist Jonah Goldberg, who echoes Michael Crichton by calling environmentalism the "Church of Green," has written about the environmental tradeoffs of reducing our dependence on oil. He writes about a "dead zone" the size of New Jersey that is destroying sea life in the Gulf of Mexico, largely the result of fertilizer runoff from American farms. He cites a 2008 study by the National Academy of Sciences finding that if we met current targets for corn-based ethanol production, we would increase the size of the "dead zone" by up to 34 percent. "Ethanol production steals precious land to produce inefficient fuel inefficiently (making food more scarce and expensive for the poor)," writes Goldberg. "If all of our transport fuel came from biofuel, we would need 30 percent more land than all of the existing food-growing farmland we have today." He notes that countries like Brazil and Malaysia are cutting down their rainforests to grow crops for biofuels; he cites a Nature Conservancy source claiming that this practice releases 17 to 420 times more carbon dioxide into the atmosphere than it offsets by reducing fossil fuel use.[142]

Goldberg also notes that wind and solar power can harm the environment by using up too much precious land. "If we tried to meet the average amount of energy typically used in America, we would need wind farms the size of Kazakhstan or solar panels the size of Spain," writes Goldberg. "Fossil fuels have been one of the great boons both to humanity and the environment, allowing forests to regrow (now that we don't use wood for heating fuel or grow fuel for horses anymore) and liberating billions from backbreaking toil. The great and permanent shortage is usable surface land and fresh water. The more land we use to produce energy, the less we have for vulnerable species, watersheds, agriculture, recreation, etc."

Goldberg wrote this column while America was suffering through the massive 2010 Gulf oil spill, caused by an accident at a deepwater BP rig. Goldberg called the spill "heartrending and tragic," but ultimately came to a conclusion that he acknowledged was counterintuitive: "[O]il is a green fuel, while 'green' fuels aren't," he wrote. "And this spill doesn't change that fact."

Also writing during the 2010 Gulf oil spill, Charles Krauthammer criticized environmental regulation:

> Here's my question: Why are we drilling in 5,000 feet of water in the first place?
>
> Many reasons, but this one goes unmentioned: Environmental chic has driven us out there. As production from the shallower Gulf of Mexico wells declines, we go deep (1,000 feet and more) and ultra deep (5,000 feet and more), in part because environmentalists have succeeded in rendering the Pacific and nearly all the Atlantic coast off-limits to oil production.... And of course, in the safest of all places, on land, we've had a 30-year ban on drilling in the Arctic National Wildlife Refuge.
>
> So we go deep, ultra deep—to such a technological frontier that no precedent exists for the...blowout in the Gulf of Mexico.
>
> There will always be catastrophic oil spills. You make them as rare as humanly possible, but where would you rather have one: in the Gulf of Mexico, upon which thousands depend for their livelihood, or in the Arctic, where there are practically no people?

> All spills seriously damage wildlife. That's a given.
> But why have we pushed the drilling from the barren
> to the populated, from the remote wilderness to a
> center of fishing, shipping, tourism and recreation?
>
> Not that the environmentalists are the only ones to
> blame. Not by far. But it is odd that they've escaped
> any mention at all.[143]

Krauthammer might have added that restricting drilling and other forms of domestic energy production requires more oil to be shipped here in tankers. "[T]hat's infinitely more dangerous, *infinitely* more dangerous—that you're going to have a major spill from a ship than you do from pipelines," said Dr. Robert Thomas, professor and director of Loyola University's Center for Environmental Communication, in a 2010 interview.[144]

It's all about tradeoffs. But you can't intelligently evaluate tradeoffs if you refuse to acknowledge that they exist.

A lot conservatives make fun of the environmentalist lifestyle— you know, the compulsive recycling, the self-righteous veganism, the earnest hybrid driving (or better yet, bicycle riding), and all the other things that activists do to reduce their carbon footprint. ConservaDave does not make fun of those people. As an ethical vegetarian, ConservaDave's lifestyle is closer to that of the environmentalists than those who mock them. And besides, ConservaDave respects people who actually make sacrifices in the hope of making the planet better. He certainly respects those people more than those who loudly advocate draconian environmental restrictions for the country as a whole, but who couldn't be bothered with the inconvenience of altering their own lifestyle.

Environmentalists have done a great service by raising the public's consciousness about the damage that we do to the planet. Their work has given us much to research, contemplate and debate. We no doubt have a cleaner environment and better health than we would have had the movement not existed. Environmental protection has thus taken its rightful place as one of many competing concerns that Americans must focus on, along with economic development, fiscal responsibility, energy independence and a host of other issues. Environmentalism can hold its own in the robust national debate, and Americans can be trusted to give it its proper due. It does not need the unfair advantage of being elevated to a religion.

10 AMERICA AND THE WORLD: THE FREEDOM AGENDA AND THE WAR ON TERROR

It was bitterly cold in Washington, D.C. on January 20, 2005. It wasn't snowing, but there was still ice on the ground from a previous storm. ConservaDave stood in a huge throng of people on the National Mall, attending his first Presidential inauguration. President George W. Bush was being sworn in for a second term. That was just fine with ConservaDave; it meant that he got to keep his job as Deputy Assistant Secretary of the Interior. ConservaDave was proud to serve in the Bush Administration, and thrilled to attend the inauguration of a man who championed "compassionate conservatism." It was compassionate conservatism, of course, that helped transform Liberal Dave into ConservaDave. As he listened to President Bush's second inaugural speech, ConservaDave was reminded of other ideals that led to his transformation:

> For a half a century, America defended our own freedom by standing watch on distant borders. After the shipwreck of communism came years of relative quiet, years of repose, years of sabbatical—and then there came a day of fire.

We have seen our vulnerability—and we have seen its deepest source. For as long as whole regions of the world simmer in resentment and tyranny—prone to ideologies that feed hatred and excuse murder—violence will gather, and multiply in destructive power, and cross the most defended borders, and raise a mortal threat. There is only one force of history that can break the reign of hatred and resentment, and expose the pretensions of tyrants, and reward the hopes of the decent and tolerant, and that is the force of human freedom.

We are led, by events and common sense, to one conclusion: The survival of liberty in our land increasingly depends on the success of liberty in other lands. The best hope for peace in our world is the expansion of freedom in all the world.

America's vital interests and our deepest beliefs are now one. From the day of our Founding, we have proclaimed that every man and woman on this earth has rights, and dignity, and matchless value, because they bear the image of the Maker of Heaven and earth. Across the generations we have proclaimed the imperative of self-government, because no one is fit to be a master, and no one deserves to be a slave. Advancing these ideals is the mission that created our Nation. It is the honorable achievement of our fathers. Now it is the urgent requirement of our nation's security, and the calling of our time.

So it is the policy of the United States to seek and support the growth of democratic movements and institutions in every nation and culture, with the ultimate goal of ending tyranny in our world.[145]

ConservaDave felt a rush of idealism that he hadn't experienced since he started to believe Reagan's crazy idea that the Cold War would not be a perpetual stalemate—that freedom would actually defeat communism. Now, less than three and a half years after the September 11, 2001 attacks—the "day of fire," as Bush called it— our President was expanding Reagan's vision to one where freedom would one day rid the world of all tyranny. There was of course no concrete plan or timetable to accomplish this monumental task—the President certainly wasn't suggesting that the job would be finished in the foreseeable future—but ConservaDave was inspired by the boldness of the President's vision. It was like Reagan declaring with confidence that communism would be left of the "ash heap of history" back when virtually none of the intelligentsia shared his confidence. And President Bush was now inviting us to envision a world where all other forms of political tyranny—including the nihilistic religious fanaticism that we were fighting in the War on Terror—would one day take their place alongside communism on that ash heap.

Of course, it is hardly going out on a limb to oppose tyranny. Everybody opposes "tyranny," since everybody defines tyranny in terms of what they oppose. But Bush went further and defined the type of society that every citizen of the planet had the right to live in: one with liberty for all, governed with the consent of the governed according to the rule of law, where the rights of minorities were protected, where the rights of women were protected. These values are often dismissed as "Western" values, but the President of the United States was declaring them to be universal values. And he was declaring it the policy of the United States to support the establishment of these societies everywhere. Bush was of course not promising a massive intervention in every non-democratic country in order to bring this vision about. But he was rejecting the usual "live and let live" acquiescence that would resign much of the world's population to oppression, promising that America would do what it could, when it could, to hasten the end of that oppression.

Bush was essentially declaring that non-democratic regimes were inherently illegitimate—not because the U.S. government had the right to tell other regimes what to do, but because no regime had the moral authority to deny basic rights to its own people. The notion that democracy is universal causes many on the left reflexively to cringe: is it not the height of arrogance to impose our values on others? But then who on the left would argue that we should have excused the denial of basic rights to a black person because he happened to be born in the South during the slavery or Jim Crow eras, or in South Africa during the apartheid era? Was it wrong to impose "our values" on those racist governments? Why, then, should we excuse the denial of basic human rights to any person because he happened to be born in a country that refuses to recognize those rights?

It was actually rather remarkable for the President of the United States to declare non-democratic regimes to be illegitimate—and to do so in such strong language. America had always stood for democracy, but had also built alliances with dictators and despots in order to protect and advance its national interests. Leftists would point to that as evidence of America's hypocrisy. Conservatives would argue that an imperfect world rarely presents us with perfect choices, and America must frequently make difficult compromises in order to preserve its long-term ability to exert positive influence in the world.

ConservaDave, notwithstanding his patriotism, would find at least some merit in the leftist argument. A leftist would be right to roll his eyes at the suggestion that when America had gotten into bed with tyrants, it had been solely out of the benevolent desire to preserve its own effectiveness as a force for good in the world. No amount of lofty rhetoric could obscure the fact that the U.S., like every nation, acts in what it perceives to be its national interests.

But it is also true that America, for all the inevitable moral inconsistencies in its foreign policy, has been by far the most powerful and effective force for the advancement of freedom, democracy and human rights around the world. What would the world look like had there been no America to counter the "values" that the Soviet Union was seeking to impose upon the world, or those that violent Islamic extremists are trying to impose today? A strong America is essential to the fight against oppression around the world. That does not lend moral legitimacy to everything that we might conceivably do to protect or augment our power, but it is nonetheless true.

Bush's speech was a challenge to America's non-democratic "friends" as well as her enemies. It is hard to know whether these allies took Bush's words seriously. Bush's call for universal freedom was a long-term vision that left us plenty of wiggle room; it was not a promise to go cold turkey on maintaining alliances of convenience with unsavory regimes. But Bush strongly proclaimed America's intention to aggressively promote liberty around the world, among friend and foe alike—not only because it was the right thing to do, but because it was in our national interest. The "Freedom Agenda" was thus born.

Bush did not specifically mention any nation in his speech, other than the United States of America. It was impossible to listen to the President's address, however, without thinking of the Muslim world. The U.S. and its allies had recently deposed the ruling regimes of two Muslim nations—the Taliban in Afghanistan and Saddam Hussein's Ba'ath Party in Iraq—and about 170,000 U.S. troops were fighting in those countries at the time of the speech.[146] Would it be possible to replace those regimes with democracies?

Islamic zealots, including the Al-Qaeda terrorist group that attacked us on 9/11 and the Taliban regime that harbored them in Afghanistan, abhor democracy as an affront to Islamic law. Their interpretation of Islam is not unanimous, however, and a few non-

Arab Muslim countries—Turkey, Indonesia, Mali, Bangladesh, Senegal—could be called democracies. After toppling the Taliban, the U.S.-led coalition helped Afghanistan—also a non-Arab Muslim country—hold a presidential election in October 2004. That election, won by then-interim President Hamid Karzai, was marred by boycotts and charges of fraud.[147]

While democracy was rare in the Muslim world as a whole, it was nonexistent in the Arab Middle East—home to 18 percent of the world's Muslim population.[148] The 21 nations of the Arab world—a collection of kingdoms, emirates, military dictatorships and military-turned-civilian dictatorships—did not include a single democracy. A number of non-democratic Arab rulers had been close allies of the U.S. over the years, including Egypt's President Hosni Mubarak and the royal family of Saudi Arabia. Scholars had even coined a term, "Arab Exceptionalism," to explain that Arabs were uniquely not desirous of, and culturally ill-suited to, democracy—and hence were exceptions to the worldwide trend towards democratization.[149]

Just 10 days after Bush's second inaugural address, the theory of "Arab Exceptionalism" was put to the test. On January 30, 2005, the people of Iraq had their first opportunity to participate in a democratic election. There had been much trepidation in the run-up to the election, as Iraq had been pounded by sectarian violence reflecting ancient rivalries among Iraq's three main ethnic groups—the Shia Muslim Arab majority, followers of the same branch of Islam practiced in Iran; the Sunni Muslim Arabs, who dominated the country under ousted Sunni dictator Saddam Hussein; and the Kurds, non-Arab Muslims concentrated in the north. There was also a constant wave of bloody attacks against U.S. troops by Iraqi insurgents, including foreign Sunni fighters linked to Al-Qaeda. On Election Day, however, millions of Iraqis ignored the threats of violence and streamed out to the polls. People around the world were inspired by footage of Iraqis waiting in massive lines for the chance to vote, and then joyously waiving their purple fingers—they were required to roll their fingers in indelible ink to prevent voter fraud—as they emerged from the polls.

The election was made possible by the U.S.-led invasion of Iraq in 2003. The U.S. and its allies did not invade Iraq for the primary purpose of liberating its people from the brutality of Saddam Hussein. The principal stated purpose was to thwart the Iraqi dictator's development and stockpiling of weapons of mass destruction (WMDs), a term that includes chemical, biological and nuclear weapons. The Bush Administration argued that in the post-9/11 world, it was simply too dangerous to allow a ruthless warmonger like Saddam Hussein to have WMDs. It was noted that Saddam had supported terrorism throughout the years, and could greatly endanger world security if he ever chose to share WMDs with terrorists.

After the U.S. military ousted Saddam, of course, it was unable to find stockpiles of WMDs or evidence that Iraq had a current program to develop them. And while it was indisputable that the Iraqi strongman had used WMDs in the past—he murdered tens of thousands or more Iraqi Kurds with chemical and other weapons in the 1980s, back when he was still one of America's "allies of convenience"[150]—Saddam's supposedly current WMD program had been the strongest selling point to garner public support for the war.

The failure to find WMDs prompted an angry reaction on the left: "Bush lied, people died." However, the quality of the analysis underlying that slogan was about as impressive as the quality of the poetry. The U.S. policy of "regime change" in Iraq—that is, the policy that the U.S. should work to topple Saddam Hussein— originated under President Clinton, not President Bush.[151] The intelligence that Bush and other world leaders relied upon from American and international agencies suggested that Iraq had an active program in chemical and biological weapons, and there was the belief in some quarters that Iraq was on its way to developing nuclear weapons.[152] That intelligence was apparently mistaken, but a mistake is not a lie. It boggles the mind that Bush would have *lied* about WMDs in order to justify invading Iraq, knowing as he must have that any failure to find WMDs would be so damaging and embarrassing. For Bush to have purposely done that would have taken a unique combination of stupidity and belligerence that could only exist in the imagination of the most fanatical of Bush-bashers.

In any event, the controversy over the failure to find WMDs—as well as the steady stream of bad news coming out of the terrorist insurgency—was temporarily eclipsed by the historic election of January 2005. Columnist Charles Krauthammer wrote about the prominent Bush critics, including comedian Jon Stewart and journalist Daniel Schorr, who were forced to contemplate the possibility that Bush may have been right about the Arab yearning for democracy. And Krauthammer also wrote about those who refused to give Bush credit:

> Our intellectuals and Middle East "experts" have been telling us that Bush's grand project to democratize the region is the fantasy of a historical illiterate. Faced with the stunning Iraqi election, they went to great lengths to attribute this inconvenient yet undeniable success to the courage of the Iraqi people.
>
> This is all very nice. But this courage was rather dormant before the American invasion. It was America's overthrow of Saddam's republic of fear that gave to the Iraqi people space and air and the very possibility of expressing courage.
>
> Those now waxing rhapsodic about the courage of the natives and the beauty of people power need to ask themselves the obvious question: Why now? It is easy to get sentimental about people power. But people power does not always prevail. Indeed, it rarely prevails. It was crushed in Hungary 1956,

Czechoslovakia 1968, Tiananmen Square 1989—and Iraq 1991. Matched against tyranny at its point of maximum cruelty, people power is useless.

In the 1991 uprising, tens of thousands of Shi'ites and Kurds were killed by the raw power of Saddam's helicopters and tanks and secret police. What was different this time? No Saddam. The American army had come ashore to disarm and depose him. After the sword, it provided the shield to allow 8 million Iraqis to revel in their first exercise of democratic self-governance.[153]

Establishing a democracy may not have been our main purpose for going to war in Iraq, but it was certainly one hell of a positive byproduct. It was hard not to get caught up in the pride and enthusiasm with which the people of Iraq were exercising their newfound franchise. That first election was far from perfect, but it exceeded all expectations. It was marred primarily by a widespread Sunni boycott, but the Sunnis joined the process in time for the next election later that year.

The January 2005 elections did not solve all of Iraq's problems. Things got worse before they got better. Violence between the Sunnis and the Shia continued to escalate. Starting in 2007, though, a number of interrelated factors hugely improved the situation: a "surge" of 20,000 troops that President Bush ordered into the country to help restore security; new strategies employed by General David Petraeus to counter the insurgency; and the rise of the "Sunni Awakening," a group of former Sunni insurgents who switched sides, joined the Pentagon payroll, and turned on Al-Qaeda. Through all the ups and downs, the elections have continued on schedule with consistently high turnout.[154] The Iraqis have made remarkable progress in the development of their democracy. We can only hope and pray that this progress will continue when U.S. troops are no longer around to counter the ambitious designs of neighboring Iran.

Krauthammer, in the March 2005 column quoted above, coined the term "Arab spring" to describe a series of positive democratic developments that were occurring in the Middle East at the time—first and foremost, of course, that unforgettable Iraqi election. It turns out that Krauthammer may have been a bit ahead of his time. That incipient "Arab spring" never really hit full blossom. A few years later, though, an earth-shattering series of events would more confidently lay claim to that term.

What is now commonly known as the "Arab Spring" began in Tunisia on December 17, 2010. Mohamed Bouazizi, a jobless young graduate, had taken to selling vegetables on the street from a cart. After police seized his cart, he set fire to himself. He later died, but not before inspiring violent riots by youth who were furious at the authorities over the incident. Riots, which were extremely rare in the North African country, quickly exploded into a mass protest movement against government oppression. Less than a month later, the unthinkable happened: Zine al-Abidine Ben Ali, the 74-year-old autocrat who had ruled Tunisia for 23 years, fled the country.[155]

Tunisia is a relatively small country, but its Spring Fever would soon spread to the most populous Arab country of them all. In the days after Ben Ali's unceremonious departure from Tunisia, Egypt experienced a rash of separate incidents where individuals set themselves ablaze—suicide by fire—to protest government oppression. On January 18, 2011, Egyptian dissident Mohamed ElBaradei, former Director General of the International Atomic Energy Agency, warned that Egypt was destined for a "Tunisia-style explosion." On the same day, anti-government activists announced national "Day of Anger" protests for January 25, 2011.[156]

ElBaradei's prediction proved to be an understatement, as the "Day of Anger" raged into the next day, and for days on end after that. Protests occurred throughout the country, but Tahrir Square in

Cairo became the focal point. Huge crowds occupied the square every day, demanding the resignation of longtime dictator Hosni Mubarak. The crowds got their wish on February 11, 2011 when Mubarak resigned after 30 years in power.[157] Less than two months into the Arab Spring, popular protests had taken out two long-time dictators—including, in Mubarak, America's closest ally in the Arab world.

Libya, wedged between Tunisia on the west and Egypt on the east, would become the third domino to fall in Arab North Africa. Protests erupted in Libya days after Mubarak's resignation. Muammar Gaddafi, Libya's despotic leader since 1969, cracked down on the protests with ruthless violence. The protests developed into an armed rebellion that, with the help of NATO air support, eventually drove Gaddafi out of power and into hiding. On October 20, 2011, Gaddafi was found by the former rebel forces—and then beaten and shot to death—near his hometown of Sirte.[158]

The people of Tunisia, Egypt and Libya had all seen the images of Iraqi Arabs proudly displaying their purple fingers, free at last after decades of Saddam's savagery. One would have to twist oneself into a pretzel in order to argue that those images had nothing to do with the popular uprisings of 2011. Of course, there are those who would rather die than give George W. Bush even partial credit for anything, and such folks are indeed intent on proving that it is possible to twist the human form into a pretzel.[159] I'll leave it to them to explain why the people of these three nations, who had suffered silently under their dictators for decades, did not rise up until after the example of Iraq gave them a glimpse of what was possible.

What remains to be seen, though, is whether the Arab Spring is a true spring. Has Arab Exceptionalism been debunked as a myth? It is too soon to tell. While overthrowing a dictator is the first step to establishing a democracy, it is but the first of many steps. There needs to be freedom of speech and freedom of the press, so that competing ideas for governing society can be fully discussed without fear of retribution. There needs to be freedom of association, so that people can choose to join together to form political parties. Those political parties need time to organize and a reasonable opportunity to compete for the people's allegiance. A strong constitution needs to be in place, to prevent popularly elected leaders from sabotaging democratic mechanisms in order to prevent those mechanisms from later bringing others to power. These freedoms and mechanisms must be credibly and effectively protected by the rule of law. The rule of law must protect minorities from being driven out of the process by the tyranny of the majority. There must be security to allow all of this to function. And that security must pass the ultimate test that every democracy must pass: the ability to transfer power peacefully from one party to another.

If you think these sound like "Western" notions—and that it is somehow a manifestation of Western imperialism to expect others to adopt them—think again. According to Freedom House, countries that qualified as "free" countries in 2011 using roughly these standards included African nations such as Ghana, South Africa, Botswana, Namibia, Mali and Benin; Asian countries such as India, Indonesia (the world's most populous Muslim nation), Japan, South Korea, Taiwan and Mongolia; almost all of the Pacific island nations; almost all of the Caribbean nations (Cuba being a notable exception); most South American countries, including Brazil, Argentina, Chile, Peru and Uruguay; and Central American nations such as El Salvador, Panama and Costa Rica.[160] To call these concepts "Western" is really an insult to people all around the world who believe they have the right to govern themselves.

The concepts of democracy are embraced in almost every part of the world. But can they penetrate the Arab world? And can they survive in the broader Muslim world? Will countries that have cast off their long-entrenched dictators end up trading one form of tyranny for another? There is a real danger of that, given that

Islamist organizations are generally the only organized opposition groups that have been strong enough to survive the political repression of Arab dictatorships. When a dictatorship is overthrown, the Islamists' organization, "name identification" and extensive network (through the mosques and charities) give them a big head start over secular reformist parties that are starting from scratch. Indeed, the first popular election of the Arab Spring was won by Islamists in Tunisia.[161] That was followed several weeks later with a major electoral victory by Islamists in Egypt's first post-Mubarak parliamentary elections.[162]

The long-term goal of Islamist parties generally is not to promote democracy, but rather to impose Sharia (Islamic law, sometimes spelled as "Shari'a" or "Shariah") upon society. And Sharia, at least as interpreted by most political Islamists, is ultimately not compatible with a free, democratic and pluralistic society.

"Globally, the compelling and powerful Islamist movement obstructs democracy," writes Islamic expert Daniel Pipes. "It seeks the opposite of reform and modernization—namely, the reassertion of the Shari'a in its entirety. A jihadist like Osama bin Laden may spell out this goal more explicitly than an establishment politician like Turkey's Prime Minister Recep Tayyip Erdoğan, but both seek to create a thoroughly anti-democratic, if not totalitarian, order."[163] Erdoğan is an Islamist who came to power in Turkey through democratic elections. He has been said to represent a moderate brand of political Islam—Turkey does not ban alcohol or the wearing of bathing suits in public, for example—and the Islamic party that won the 2011 election in Tunisia has been said to be of a similar mold.[164] Pipes, however, is not as sanguine about Erdoğan nor, presumably, about other supposedly moderate Islamists:

> Islamists respond two ways to democracy. First, they denounce it as un-Islamic. Muslim Brotherhood founder Hasan al-Banna considered democracy a

betrayal of Islamic values. Brotherhood theoretician Sayyid Qutb rejected popular sovereignty, as did Abu al-A'la al-Mawdudi, founder of Pakistan's Jamaat-e-Islami political party. Yusuf al-Qaradawi, Al-Jazeera television's imam, argues that elections are heretical.

Despite this scorn, Islamists are eager to use elections to attain power, and have proven themselves to be agile vote-getters; even a terrorist organization (Hamas) has won an election [in Gaza]. This record does not render the Islamists democratic but indicates their tactical flexibility and their determination to gain power. As Erdoğan has revealingly explained, "Democracy is like a streetcar. When you come to your stop, you get off."[165]

The Muslim Brotherhood, which Pipes refers to above, was founded in Egypt in 1928. According to the Council on Foreign Relations, the Muslim Brotherhood is "Egypt's oldest and largest Islamist organization," is "widely considered to be the world's most influential Islamist organization, with numerous branches and affiliates," and "has emerged as Egypt's biggest opposition movement." The group has a legacy of violence:

Sayyid Qutb, a prominent member of the Brotherhood, laid down the ideological ground for the use of jihad, or armed struggle, against the regime in Egypt and beyond. Qutb's writings, in particular his 1964 work *Milestones*, has provided the intellectual and theological underpinnings for the founders of numerous radical and militant Islamist groups, including al-Qaeda. Extremist leaders often channel Qutb to argue that governments not ruled by sharia are apostate and, therefore, legitimate targets of jihad.

The Muslim Brotherhood's commitment to imposing Sharia through the force of arms is reflected in slogans such as "Islam is the solution" and "jihad is our way." [166]

Radical Islam presents numerous dilemmas for liberals, pitting some of their most cherished ideals against one another—and forcing them to choose sides in battles that they want no part of. Liberalism is the home of modern feminism, for example. Sharia is antithetical to feminism. The various forms of gender discrimination under Sharia are well known: Men are allowed to take up to four wives, but women are allowed only one husband. A woman cannot initiate divorce against her husband, but a man can divorce his wife merely by saying "I divorce you!" three times. Muslim men can marry outside of the faith; Muslim women cannot. A woman's testimony is worth half that of a man. If a woman loses her virginity before marriage or is suspected of having a romantic relationship with a non-Muslim, it is considered a stain on the family's honor. The men of the family typically restore that honor (in their view) by murdering the girl—"honor killings" that are rarely prosecuted. Honor killings are also common against women who have lost their virginity because of rape. Men, on the other hand, are encouraged to have premarital sex. [167]

While women are second-class citizens throughout the Muslim world, the degree of discrimination against them varies from place to place. The Taliban regime in Afghanistan was particularly brutal on women: women were forbidden to work, go to school, drive, or move around freely in public. [168] Saudi Arabia, supposedly a U.S. ally, also forbids women to drive. Each woman in Saudi Arabia is required to have a male guardian, whose permission is required for that woman to travel, get an education, get a job, open a bank account, or get married. A strict dress code, similar to that which was enforced by the Taliban, requires all Saudi women to appear almost completely covered in public. [169] In Islamic (and some non-Islamic) countries in Africa, female genital mutilation is routinely inflicted on girls as a way of eliminating their sexual desire. In its most extreme form, all of the external genitalia are cut off and the area is stitched together, leaving only a small opening for menstruation and intercourse.[170]

Although the Taliban was driven from power in Afghanistan in 2001, the oppression of women in that country continued. In 2011, Afghan President Karzai announced the pardoning of a teenage girl that had been sentenced to 12 years in prison for having sex out of wedlock. That the sex had not been voluntary—she had been raped by a relative—was not relevant under Afghan law. The judge had previously offered the girl freedom *if she would agree to marry the rapist.* She refused. Karzai's pardon came only after the victim ultimately relented and agreed to marry her attacker.[171]

One would expect that the treatment of women in the Islamic world—even the less extreme forms of discrimination that prevail in more permissive Muslim societies—would outrage feminists in the West. The problem, though, is that most Western feminists are also liberals, and in liberalism, the highest sin is to be judgmental (except against political conservatives). And the paramount sin is to be judgmental against another culture—or, more accurately, against a "Third World" culture. Under the leftist narrative of Western oppression, a Third World culture such as Islam is automatically granted the noble and protected status of victimhood. This creates the presumption that Westerners who criticize such a culture are racist, a charge that is the ultimate humiliation for any liberal. (Conservatives are used to being called racist, but don't much enjoy it either.)

It is actually an admirable liberal trait to give other cultures the benefit of the doubt, and to take no joy in putting down other cultures. Liberals in this way present a contrast to those who seem to believe, in tribalistic fashion, that their culture is perfect. This trait in liberals is a good one when it is born out of humility and open-mindedness, but a bad one when it is born out of cultural self-loathing or misplaced guilt. Some Western leftists appear to take their non-tribalism to an extreme, hating to admit that there's anything good about the culture they were born into. At that point, it's no longer about humility and open-mindedness, and the people who get to that point tend to lack both traits.

For whatever psychological motivation, American feminists have been much more vociferous in their condemnation of "male chauvinist pigs" in their own country than the oppressors of women in the Islamic world, even though the sins of the former are insignificant in comparison to the sins of the latter. It almost suggests a mystifying lack of compassion for their "sisters" who, through no fault of their own, happen to have been born into another culture. And that seems to be rather un-liberal.

Some well-meaning liberals will deflect criticism of Muslim discrimination against women by noting the many centuries that various horrible things were tolerated in the Christian world. "It took Christian civilization two thousand years to evolve away from our own barbaric practices, and we're still far from perfect," the argument goes. "Muslim societies are going through the same modernization process that we had to go through."

That may be true, but we have to protect human rights according to international norms as they have progressed to the present time. How, for example, would we react if we discovered that some other culture was practicing slavery today? We would condemn it and hopefully try to end it. We wouldn't just shrug our shoulders and say well, we Americans used to do that kind of thing ourselves 150 years ago. And *of course* we're still not perfect. But if one had to be perfect in order to have the moral authority to criticize others for perpetrating injustice, then every single liberal (and non-liberal) activist would be muzzled.

For Western feminists to acknowledge the plight of oppressed Muslim women requires them to also acknowledge the tension between their two cherished ideals of feminism and multiculturalism. Some may pretend not to see the oppression, in order to avoid facing the contradictions among the various strains of their political belief system. One liberal feminist who is willing to face down those contradictions is author Susan Jacoby. She has taken her fellow liberals to task for failing to stand up for Ayaan Hirsi Ali, a Muslim-born activist who has risked her life to campaign for women's rights in the Islamic world. Jacoby writes:

> I am an atheist with an affinity for non-fundamentalist religious believers whose faith has made room for secular knowledge. I am also a political liberal. I am not, however, a multiculturalist who believes that all cultures and religions are equally worthy of respect. And I find myself in a lonely place in relation to many liberals, political and religious, because I cannot accept a multiculturalism that tends to excuse, under the rubric of "tolerance," religious and cultural practices that violate universal human rights.

> The latest example of the Left's blind spot on this issue is the antagonism of so many liberal reviewers toward Ayaan Hirsi Ali's recent memoir, *Nomad.* The Somali-born Hirsi Ali immigrated to the United States in 2006 after her close friend, the Dutch film director Theo Van Gogh, was murdered by a radical Islamist. Hirsi Ali still needs bodyguards because of frequent death threats.

> She was educated as a child in Muslim schools, subjected to genital mutilation, and broke with her family when she refused to consent to an arranged marriage. She first settled in Holland, where she worked as a Somali-Dutch interpreter, and her convictions about violence in many (though not, she emphasizes, all) Muslim families are rooted in her

work with immigrants as well as her own upbringing. Yet Nicholas D. Kristof, reviewing *Nomad* for the *New York Times Book Review*, writes that "I couldn't help thinking that perhaps Hirsi Ali's family is dysfunctional simply because its members never learned to bite their tongues and just say to one another: 'I love you.'"

I was startled by this patronizing comment, because I admire Kristof for being one of the few male columnists who writes frequently about violence against women. Somehow, "I love you" isn't the first thing that would come to mind if I were being held down by female relatives while my clitoris was maimed or if my father told me I had to marry a stranger.[172]

Kristof's gratuitous snark about a woman of such great courage seemed so inappropriately off-the-wall that it had me wondering: "Where did *that* come from?" Perhaps it came from the same place as the following "observation" about Hirsi Ali, as reported in *The Washington Post*: "Neoconservative, middle-aged white men, Dutch author Ian Buruma noted, tend to swoon when she walks into the room. Muslim women of her complexion, whom she says she wants to rescue from Islamic oppression, tend to recoil."[173] For those of you unfamiliar with leftist code-speak, "white men" have very little credibility, "*middle-aged* white men" have even less, and "*neoconservative*, middle-aged white men" have none at all. A woman of Ayaan Hirsi Ali's dark complexion, on the other hand, has tremendous credibility—unless, presumably, she happens to be Ayaan Hirsi Ali herself. Buruma was thus instructing us to conclude that the "swooning" is to be mocked, and that the correct response to Hirsi Ali is indeed to recoil.

In her feminist activism, Hirsi Ali has been a blunt critic of Islam. For that sin, she requires the constant protection of bodyguards. Whether they agree or disagree with her critiques of her former religion, Western leftists should be in awe of how Hirsi Ali has put her life on the line to fight for the rights of women. In that context, the remarks of Kristof and Buruma seem absurdly trivial and even bitchy—the passive-aggressive sniping of weak men who lack the moral authority to take this woman on directly, and so instead try to pull her down with snide comments. She clearly makes them uncomfortable. Perhaps it is because she has been embraced by conservatives (after liberals shunned her), as if the sin of associating with those who think differently cancels out her heroic efforts to protect oppressed women. Perhaps it is because she upsets the narratives that leftists use to explain all of the world's ills—a narrative where the villains must always be "neoconservative, middle aged white men." Perhaps it is because she puts them in the uncomfortable position of having to choose between their supposed feminism and their supposed multiculturalism—again upsetting their narrative, where the oppressed peoples of the world are united in common cause against their Western oppressors. Or perhaps it is because her bravery shames them in their cowardice, and in their impotent inability to climb out of their politically correct box to support people who need it.

Women are not the only ones who face discrimination in the Islamic world. Religious minorities and gays are oppressed as well. "Nowhere in the world is bigotry so rampant as in Muslim countries," writes Hirsi Ali. "No difference is greater between American and Islamic principles than the founding ideals of both. It is on the basis of the founding ideals of Islam that al-Qa'ida and other Muslim puritans insist on the implementation of sharia law, jihad and the eternal subjection of women. It is on the basis of the founding ideals of America that blacks and women fought for—and gained—equal rights and gays and new immigrants continue to do so."[174]

This is presumably the type of unabashed judgmentalism that causes Western leftists to "recoil" at Hirsi Ali. The judgmentalism is objectionable because it is directed in the "wrong" direction: at a Third World culture in an unfavorable comparison to America. For an African woman to make such a judgment is considered a racial apostasy by hardcore (white) Western leftists, as infuriating as her religious apostasy was to those who would put her to death for it. Western leftists would not sentence Hirsi Ali to death for her apostasy, but would instead seek to strip her of the nobility and credibility conferred by her dark skin—insinuating that she had essentially become a "middle aged white male" and hence her views could be dismissed.

Religious bigotry in the Muslim world, like the gender oppression that exists there, causes conflict in the belief systems of Western liberals. Liberals profess tolerance of the cultural and religious practices of others—generally a good thing—but does that require them to be tolerant of practices that are themselves intolerant? Most liberals would say no, but would still feel uneasy about criticizing practices that fell under the protective veil of a minority community's "culture." They would therefore not condone the hatred of Hindus, Jews, Christians and others that is rampant in the Muslim world, but might seek to minimize it by noting that every religion has its share of bigots and extremists. They would likely resist the conclusion that bigotry and extremism is a bigger problem in the Islamic world than elsewhere, perhaps drawing a moral equivalence with Christian fundamentalists in America.

Western liberals instinctively have a politically correct aversion to criticizing any "community of color," even when such communities behave in ways that violate fundamental liberal ideals. Perhaps that is driven, at least in part, by a laudable concern that negative generalizations about any minority community might lead, as they have in the past, to discrimination. More extreme Western leftists, on the other hand, have additional motivation to whitewash the bigotry and misogyny that exists in much of the Muslim community. They secretly admire the way that radical Muslims violently attack the Western institutions that leftists hate. The radical leftists see Muslim extremists as proxies for themselves, embodying the rage that the leftists viscerally feel at the power structures of their own societies. The Western radicals dare not express their rage in the violent manner that Muslim terrorists do, because they rely upon the freedoms and comforts provided by the institutions that they despise. But the hardcore leftists, at least at some level, revere the hardcore Islamists for doing what the Western leftists dare not do.

This might explain why the left appears to afford Muslims a preferred status among communities of color. It was fairly predictable, for example, that the white British filmmakers of *Slumdog Millionaire* would choose to make their hero a Muslim who was persecuted by Indian Hindus. Those scenarios certainly exist in India, where ethnic tensions among impoverished communities sometimes result in violence. Hindus sometimes attack Muslims in India, but Muslims give at least as good as they get.[175] And almost 180 million Muslims vote with their feet by choosing to live in India,[176] rather than seeking "refuge" in Pakistan—which was created to be a Muslim homeland within the former British colonial boundaries of India. India, the world's largest democracy, not only has the third largest population of Muslims in the world, but is also home to many thriving religious minority communities—Sikhs, Christians, Buddhists, Jains, Zoroastrians, Jews, and many others. Pakistan, on the other hand, is a very inhospitable environment for religious minorities. The land now occupied by Pakistan was home to millions of Hindus, Sikhs and others before India was partitioned to create the Muslim state; the negligible number of non-Muslims who remain on the Pakistan side of the partition is a stark contrast to the vibrant religious diversity that flourishes on the Indian side. In spite of Hindu India's much stronger (albeit flawed) record on the prized leftist value of "multiculturalism," the Western left (particularly the British left, which has more of an historical interest in South Asia) tends to be more sympathetic to Muslims than to Hindus. Was it a big deal that the makers of *Slumdog Millionaire* would portray a Muslim as being the victim of Hindu oppression? No. But as noted above, it was highly predictable.

Liberals are right, however, that we need to protect Muslims living in our midst from discrimination. That is a noble sentiment. In the wake of 9/11, many feared a vigilante backlash against American Muslims. Fortunately, that backlash never materialized: In 2010, Muslims were the victims of 13.2 percent of the religiously motivated hate crimes in the U.S. but Jews were the victims of 65.4 percent—more than five-and-a-half times as many.[177] (Jews have consistently been the targets of the large majority of religiously motivated hate crimes in the U.S., accounting for 70 percent in 2009 and 66 percent in 2008.) The U.S. government under both the Bush and Obama Administrations has gone to great pains to stress that we are not at war with Islam or with the Muslim people, and has made strenuous efforts to avoid rhetoric that might offend Muslims or incite antipathy against them.

The effort to avoid needlessly offending Muslims is commendable. We have arguably taken that effort to the point, however, where we are dangerously obscuring who we are fighting and why. The Obama Administration rewrote the U.S. National Security Strategy to purge it of terms like "Islamic radicalism," and has propagated a new set of rules on how the government is to refer to our post-9/11 military and intelligence efforts. We are not supposed to describe groups like Al-Qaeda, or the terrorism that they employ, as "Islamic" or "Muslim"—even though the terrorists embrace those labels and are clearly motivated by their extreme interpretation of Islam. We are not allowed to say that they are engaged in "jihad" against us, even though *they* claim that they are waging jihad against us. We are not allowed to say that our enemies seek to establish a worldwide "caliphate" (Islamic regime governed according to Sharia), even though *they* clearly state that their goal is to establish a worldwide caliphate.[178] It's almost as if our enemies are intent on telling us the truth and our own government is equally intent on not telling us the truth.

I understand what the objective is here. We don't want the large majority of Muslims who are peaceful to think that we're at war with them or their religion. That makes sense. But whom do we think we're fooling? It's almost humorous to see our mostly Christian leaders tell Islamic radicals—who have devoted their entire lives to studying their religion—that they're not true Muslims and have completely misinterpreted Islam. That is not to say that the radicals *are* true Muslims or that they have *not* misinterpreted Islam, but those of us who are outside of the faith should have the humility to stay out of that conversation. I give the faith the benefit of the doubt and assume that the terrorists are practicing a grotesque perversion of Islam. I definitely want to believe that, but I don't have the expertise to know that with any great certainty. And I'm certainly not going to presume to instruct any Muslim on the proper interpretation of his religion.

The problem with this rampant political correctness is that we are likely failing to fool Muslims but are succeeding in fooling ourselves. There is a real danger that the American public will fail to understand who our enemies are, what motivates them, and why we're fighting. That confusion can only undermine our chances of success. Even the term "War on Terror" is an obfuscation of who our enemy is. Terrorism, as many have pointed out, is a tactic; we can't be at war with a tactic. Obama made things even less clear by dropping the term "War on Terror" without replacing it with anything. The U.S. National Security Strategy had previously identified our enemy as "the transnational terrorists [who] exploit the proud religion of Islam to serve a violent political vision." The Obama Administration struck those words, and identified our enemy as "violent extremism."[179] That term is broad enough to pick up Basque terrorists, the Tamil Tigers in Sri Lanka, the Irish Republican Army, the Shining Path guerillas in Peru, numerous militia groups in Africa, and countless other armed extremists who, although engaged in deplorable acts, are not a threat to America. If you want to get technical, the term is also broad enough to include any protestor with extreme political views who so much as throws a rock or bottle at the police—including a few of the Occupy Wall Street protestors. Hopefully, the folks at the Pentagon and Homeland Security are secretly provided with a little more specificity about whom we're supposed to be fighting. But the general public is left only with the lame euphemism "violent extremism." And it's hard to get the public to rally around a euphemism.

Connecticut Senator Joseph Lieberman improves Obama's term greatly by simply adding one word. Lieberman defines our enemy as "violent *Islamist* extremism."[180] "Islamist," as opposed to "Islamic," refers to those who see Islam not only as a religion but also as a political system. We are at war with practitioners of an extremist version of political Islam who use violence to impose their will upon others. These are people who, when given the chance, brutally oppress women, gays and anyone who does not subscribe to their religious views. These are the people who declared war on us before we declared war on them. We are not at war with the religion of Islam or Muslims in general. We are at war with a small but dangerous percentage of the people who call themselves Muslims, and who claim that Islam is the basis for the violence they perpetrate and the oppression they seek to impose.

Many so-called experts assert that the "root cause" of violent Islamist extremism is the conflict between Israel and Palestine. This is said to be a major source of Muslim grievances against the West— particularly the U.S., which has supported Israel's right to exist and to defend itself.[181] This view is nonsensical on its face. For one thing, Islamic extremists are not just at war with the "West." They are in conflict with virtually every type of non-Muslim community—and even many Muslim communities—with which they interact. Does the conflict between Israel and Palestine really explain the violent conflicts between Muslims and Hindus in South Asia? Between Muslims and Buddhists in Thailand? Between Muslims and Christians in Nigeria, the Philippines, Chechnya, Cyprus, Kosovo, Bosnia and Macedonia? Does the Israel-Palestine conflict explain the recent Muslim massacres of Christians in Côte d'Ivoire, or the recent genocidal ethnic cleansing of Christians by Muslims in Sudan and Timor-Leste?[182] Would solving the Israel-Palestine conflict really cause the "grievances" that animate those other conflicts to evaporate?

This notion that the Israel-Palestine conflict is somehow the "root cause" of Islamic extremism is just one of commonly mouthed narratives about that conflict that does not survive scrutiny. Israel is often portrayed, particularly by the left, as a white colonialist outpost in the Middle East. Many would be surprised to learn that the Jewish population of Israel is largely non-white. Until recently, about 70 percent of Israel's Jews were Middle Eastern Jews— descendents of Jews who continued to live in the Middle East from the time of their ancient expulsion from Israel, and who have hence retained the brown skin and Middle Eastern features that they share with their Arab "cousins." (Jews and Arabs are both descendents of Abraham.) The population of Israel's European Jews—that is, descendents of the Jews who eventually found their way into Europe after being evicted from Israel, and whose complexion and features have been diluted from intermixing with Europeans over the centuries—recently caught up to that of the Middle Eastern Jews due to a massive wave of immigration from Russia.[183]

The Middle Eastern Jews lived as persecuted minorities in Muslim countries for centuries. The situation worsened for Jews in the 20th century with the rise of Arab nationalism. Judaism was virtually outlawed in much of the Middle East. In 1945, prior to the establishment of the State of Israel, the Arab League declared that "Jewish products and manufactured goods shall be considered undesirable to the Arab countries."[184] In 1948, after the Arab League declared all Jewish people enemy citizens, the persecution of Jews living in Arab lands intensified: "Jewish bank accounts and property were confiscated, Jews were arrested and fired from their jobs, and synagogues were attacked. Homes were looted, women were raped and people were killed."[185] Since 1940, approximately 1,000,000 Jews have fled brutal oppression in Arab lands—or were forcibly expelled from communities that they had inhabited since ancient times. Israel provided a refuge for most of them, and millions of Jews in Israel are the descendents of those who fled persecution in the Muslim world.

Helen Thomas, one of the most prominent American journalists, opined to an interviewer in 2010 that Jews should "get the hell out of Palestine." It is clear from the context that "Palestine," as she defined it, included the State of Israel. The interviewer then asked Thomas where the Jews should go. "They can go home," she said, to "Poland, Germany, America, and everywhere else."[186]

One might ask Thomas whether millions of Israeli Middle Eastern Jews should go "home" to Muslim nations that are diseased with the most virulent Jew hatred that exists in the world—countries that expelled them, seized their property, murdered their ancestors and outlawed their religion. And the Jew hatred in these nations is not just an unfortunate artifact of history; it is alive and well and should turn the stomach of every self-respecting liberal.

"Several Arab governments provide their people cradle-to-grave indoctrination in raw anti-Semitism," writes Nina Shea of the Hudson Institute's Center for Religious Freedom. "Their education systems, government media, and state-financed clergy bombard citizens with the view that Jews must be hated."[187] She gives several examples, including Saudi schools instructing children that Jews "obey the devil"; a television series aired throughout the Muslim world depicting a Jews making matzo (Jewish unleavened bread) with the blood of Muslims and Christians, and plotting to rule the world; posters and cartoons throughout the Muslim world depicting Jews eating children; and Arab schools and media routinely teaching or reporting, as if it were fact, maliciously fabricated anti-Jewish propaganda that the Nazis and Czarist Russians once used to justify the murder of Jews.

This disgusting bigotry is not merely a project of Muslim governments; it has taken deep root among the people. Shea notes that in a recent demonstration in Berlin, Middle Eastern immigrants invoked the old European "blood libel" myth against Jews by chanting: "Israel drinks the blood of our children." CBS News correspondent Lara Logan was savagely beaten, stripped and sexually assaulted for 30 minutes by a crowd of "Arab Spring" demonstrators in Cairo as the frenzied mob around her chanted, "Jew! Jew! Jew!"[188]

Not that it matters, but Lara Logan is not Jewish. For people who really are Jewish, sending them "home" to the murderous hatred their parents fled in the Muslim world would be tantamount to a death sentence. Helen Thomas may have been speaking as a leftist when she implored Israel's Jews to "go home," but she certainly wasn't speaking as a liberal. No genuine liberal could ever have the heart to resign Israel's Middle Eastern Jews to such a fate. Those who question Israel's right to exist are questioning the right of millions of Middle Eastern Jews to be protected from horrendous persecution. It is the existence of Israel that allows these Jews to live in the region that they have lived in continuously for thousands of years without having to endure such persecution.

The intention here is not to suggest that Muslims are generally bigoted. That itself would be a bigoted statement; it would not be fair to multitudes of decent people. But governments, cultural institutions and religious institutions throughout the Muslim world have created a climate of rampant bigotry that makes it virtually impossible for Jewish minorities to live in Muslim nations. Israel, the only Jewish-majority nation in the world, is thus a necessary refuge for Middle Eastern Jews. Ironically, the Muslim leaders who so stridently oppose the existence of Israel are the ones most responsible for making Israel indispensible.

If the Islamists and leftists who deny Israel's right to exist were morally and logically consistent, they would also deny Pakistan's right to exist. On their way out the door as the colonial rulers of India, the British arranged for the partition of India into two countries: India and Pakistan. (Pakistan included two noncontiguous parts, and the eastern part would later split off to become the independent nation of Bangladesh.) The partition was effected in the name of Muslim self-determination: Muslims would be given a homeland in two parts of India where they constituted a majority. In order to make room for the Muslim homeland, however, over 7 million Hindus and Sikhs had to vacate their ancestral homelands,[189] the cradle of their respective civilizations. The logic of partition was essentially as follows: Everyone was entitled to stay in the region but, in order to create a Muslim state alongside a multicultural Hindu-majority state, many people would move from one part of the region to another. If your particular village or region was within the borders of the "other side," you could still exercise your right of self-determination by moving "next door" to rejoin "your side."

Shortly after the partition of India, the United Nations approved a plan to partition Palestine (which was then ruled by the British under a U.N. mandate) into a Jewish state and an Arab state. In 1948, Israel declared its independence and was promptly attacked by the armies of five Arab nations: Egypt, Syria, Jordan, Lebanon and Iraq. Their intention was to "drive the Jews into the sea," leaving all of Palestine for the Arabs. "It will be a war of annihilation," Azzam

Pasha, Secretary-General of the Arab League, enthused at the time. "It will be a momentous massacre in history that will be talked about like the massacres of the Mongols or the Crusades."[190]

The Arab armies failed to drive the Jews into the sea. Israel signed separate armistice agreements with the Arab nations in 1949 and 1950, resulting in Jordan controlling what is now called the West Bank, Egypt controlling the Gaza Strip, and Israel controlling the rest of Palestine. About 630,000 Arab refugees from Palestine[191] were kept mostly in the West Bank and Gaza. Israel would seize control of the West Bank and Gaza in the Six-Day War of June 1967. In the almost two decades that those territories were controlled by Jordan and Egypt, respectively, those countries made no effort to establish a Palestinian state there—nor were they pressured by Palestinian activists, the left or the international community to do so.

Most reasonable people now believe that the Israeli-Palestinian conflict should be settled through a "land-for-peace" arrangement whereby a Palestinian state would be established on land conquered by Israel in 1967. This would be a "reset" of the partition concept that was attempted in the 1940s, albeit with different borders. Israel should not withdraw completely to its pre-1967 borders, which after all are only armistice lines. Those borders are not defensible; they would leave Israel only nine miles wide at its narrowest point, squeezed precariously between the Palestinian state and the Mediterranean Sea.[192] Many details would have to be worked out through painful negotiation, but the concept of a new partition—a "two-state solution"—is the only viable path to peace.

Most Islamists and many on the left do not support a two-state solution. They insist on a one-state solution, because they deny Israel's right to exist. Therein lies their hypocrisy. They regard the establishment of Pakistan as a good thing, even though it caused over 7 million Hindus and Sikhs to be displaced from their ancestral homeland in the name of Muslim self-determination. They regard the establishment of Israel as evil, because it caused a much smaller number of Arabs to be displaced in the name of Jewish self-determination. The establishment of Israel allowed about a million Middle Eastern Jews to find freedom by moving in from "next door"—the various Muslim countries in the region that had oppressed them. Similarly, the establishment of post-partition India allowed millions of Hindus and Sikhs to escape the difficult life of a religious minority in a Muslim country by moving in from "next-door" Pakistan—just as the establishment of Pakistan allowed Muslims to realize their dream of self-determination by moving in from "next-door" India.

A two-state solution will also allow Palestinians to realize their dream of self-determination. Those whose ancestral villages are within the Palestinian state will be able to live in those villages. Those whose ancestral villages are within Israel will claim their self-determination by living "next door." That is how partition worked for India and Pakistan, and that is how it will work for Israel and Palestine.

And regarding the "ancestral" villages of the Palestinians: It is a myth that the people we now call "Palestinians" have an ancient and unbroken tie to Palestine, and were displaced by Jews who returned after a complete absence of almost 2,000 years. There had never been a Palestinian state. Although the first major wave of Jewish migration to Palestine under Zionism (the Jewish nationalist movement) started in the 1890s, Jews had maintained a continuous presence in the Holy Land since ancient times and Jerusalem has had a Jewish majority since 1860.[193] Many if not most of those now identified as "Palestinians" migrated to Palestine from other parts of the Arab world *after* returning Jews had settled there. They were attracted by the economic activity created by Jewish settlement. And contrary to the Islamist and leftist narrative, Jewish settlement did not throw Palestinians who were already there off their land. The land was very sparsely populated when the Jewish settlers began to arrive. The Jews settled land that was either vacant and unclaimed, or that was purchased from absentee landlords.[194] The Jews did not rule Palestine (the Ottoman Turks did during the first major Zionist migration), and did not have the authority or the ability to throw anyone off their land.

Not only had there never been a Palestinian state, but Palestinians have not, until recently, thought of themselves as a distinct people within the Arab nation. The historic borders of Palestine, under the United Nations mandate, included not only Israel, Gaza and the West Bank, but also all of Jordan. In the 1920s, the British lopped off 78 percent of Palestine to establish an emirate for one of their Arab allies.[195] That ally, Abdullah, was not from Palestine; he was from Arabia (now Saudi Arabia). Abdullah went on to found the Kingdom of Jordan on his part of historic Palestine. Had there been a Palestinian national identity—as distinct from the general Arab identity—then Abdullah would have been regarded as a foreign monarch on Palestinian soil. If Palestinians and their supporters deny the legitimacy of Jewish sovereignty over less than 22 percent of Palestine, why do they not also challenge the legitimacy of a foreign monarchy's sovereignty over 78 percent of Palestine? The answer is that Palestinians did not think of themselves as a separate nationality; Abdullah and his progeny were merely Arab rulers ruling Arab—as opposed to Palestinian—land.

Similarly, when Egypt controlled Gaza and Jordan controlled the West Bank, those areas were never referred to as the "Occupied Territories." But why would non-Palestinian Egyptians and non-Palestinian Jordanians not be considered occupiers of Palestinian land? The answer, again, is that there was no Palestinian identity separate and distinct from Arab identity. The Egyptians and the Jordanians were merely Arabs controlling Arab land, and no one—not even the Palestinians—complained about their failure to establish a Palestinian state on that land when they had the chance.

But if there was no separate Palestinian national identity, what would be the need for a separate Palestinian state? There are already over 20 Arab states. If Palestinians were merely Arabs, then they could be absorbed into the existing Arab states, just as Hindus displaced from Pakistan could be absorbed into India. That is the principle of partition. The truth is that a separate Palestinian national identity did not emerge until after the Palestine Liberation Organization was formed in 1964. Palestinian nationalism is thus a much more recent phenomenon than Zionism, its Jewish counterpart. Ironically, Palestinian nationalism would likely not have appeared had it not been for Zionism. But it did appear.

The Palestinians have undermined their claim to a distinct national identity by never seeking the "liberation" of all of Palestine, but only of that portion of Palestine that happened to be controlled by the Jews at any given time. But despite its logical inconsistencies and relatively short history, Palestinian nationalism is now firmly established and is not going anywhere. Zionism is also firmly established and is not going anywhere. The Jews and Palestinians who support their respective national movements are also not going anywhere. A two-state solution is likely the only solution. But it is a solution that is only possible if the Islamists in the entire region—not just in Palestine—truly abandon their dream of "driving the Jews into the sea."

Israel is a miniscule sliver of land in the middle of an enormous region filled with those who are bent on its destruction. In that hostile environment, the compromises required of Israel to make peace can be rendered impossible because of the steps required of Israel to protect its security. Israel faces real threats to its survival as a nation on a daily basis, and survival must always trump all other priorities.

The so-called experts, as usual, have gotten it backwards. The Israel-Palestine conflict is not the cause of violent Islamist extremism, and hence resolving that conflict will not defeat violent

Islamist extremism. It is violent Islamist extremism that must be defeated in order to resolve the Israel-Palestine conflict, and countless other conflicts around the globe.

The current regime in Iran is the most active state sponsor of terrorism in the world.[196] Iranian President Mahmoud Ahmadinejad has unleashed a steady torrent of hateful and threatening rhetoric against Israel and the Jewish people, proclaiming that "Israel must be wiped off the map," and that the "Islamic world will not let its historic enemy live in its heartland." Ahmadinejad, who could not speak without the approval of the religious mullahs who really run Iran, vehemently denies that the Nazis murdered 6 million Jews during World War II—which seems strange, because he would clearly not be offended by the mass slaughter of Jews. What does offend Ahmadinejad, presumably, is that European persecution of Jews might somehow justify the existence of the hated State of Israel. But what really justifies the existence of Israel is the persecution of Jews in Muslim lands by hate-mongers like Ahmadinejad. Iran is intent on acquiring nuclear weapons so that it can make good on its threats. In spite of his war-like rhetoric, though, Ahmadinejad has offered his own plan for "peace in the Middle East": the destruction of Israel.[197] Ahmadinejad has thus revealed the all-purpose peace plan for violent Islamist extremists everywhere, whether they be fighting Jews, Christians, Hindus, Sikhs, Buddhists, animists or other infidels: destroy your enemies.

This is what Israel is up against, and this is what all decent people are up against. This is clearly a clash of world views, and the violent Islamist extremist world view holds absolutely no room for anything that liberals hold dear. Just as communism could never have been defeated without an assertive and strong America, the fanatical hatred spewed by the likes of Ahmadinejad cannot be defeated without an assertive and strong America.

Liberals have a healthy aversion to the use of force, but force is sometimes unavoidable when dealing with an enemy that seeks to violently impose its repressive theology on others. "We can try to imagine a world of diplomats without soldiers, but it would be no more peaceful than a society of therapists without policemen," wrote Michael Gerson, former speechwriter for President George W. Bush. "Coercion is not the ultimate source of peace—but peace is sometimes unachievable without it."[198] Conservatives recognize this more instinctively, but when push comes to shove, liberals are also willing to use force to defend American values and universal values.

The late author and journalist Christopher Hitchens, an atheist and self-described Marxist, riled many of his fellow leftists with his support for the War on Terror. After a Hitchens speech in 2007, a questioner from the audience said that he was "very much troubled" by Hitchens' remarks about "the need to stand up and fight against this Muslim jihad." The questioner referred to the "crimes" that were being committed by the U.S. in Iraq and Afghanistan, and asserted that the violent acts of the Islamists were merely "the response to the crimes of U.S. and European imperialism." Responding in his typical take-no-prisoners fashion, Hitchens explained why the rest of the world had an obligation to fight the violent Islamist extremists:

> If you want to avoid upsetting these people, you have to let Indonesia commit genocide in East Timor, otherwise they'll be upset with you. You'll have made an enemy. If you tell them they can't throw acid in the faces of unveiled women in Karachi, they will be annoyed with you. If you say we insist, we think cartoonists in Copenhagen can print satire on the Prophet Mohammad, you've just made an enemy. You've brought it on. You're encouraging it to happen.
>
> So unless you are willing to commit suicide for yourself and for this culture, get used to the compromises you will have to make and the eventual

capitulation that will come to you. But bloody well don't do that in my name because I'm not doing it. You surrender in your own name. Leave me out of it.

I am going to fight these people and every other theocrat *all the way*. All the way. For free expression, for women's rights, for self-determination of small peoples, for the right of Iraqis to federate and have their own show, for the right of the Lebanese to not be bullied by Hezbollah and to have a multi-cultural democracy.

Yes, I'll fight for this and I think the 82nd Airborne is brave to be fighting for it too. I think you should be ashamed for sneering at people who guard you while you sleep.[199]

With notable exceptions like Christopher Hitchens, the most hardcore leftists have been trapped by their hatred of the West into being apologists for the most illiberal of practices, including misogyny, bigotry, religious intolerance, and tyranny. Liberals must not fall into the same trap.

11 A HOPEFUL, YOUTHFUL, IDEALISTIC AND OPTIMISTIC CONSERVATISM

Some may find it provocative to suggest that conservative policies are the best way to achieve liberal ideals. I have tried to explain why that is true by discussing several issues. Of course, "liberal ideals" encompass many things, and they often clash with one another. A key to the thesis of this book is that tradeoffs always exist—tradeoffs between protecting the environment and creating jobs; between income equality and economic growth; between protecting unions and protecting schoolchildren; between regulation and efficiency; between feminism and multiculturalism; between spending for today's needs and ensuring that our children and grandchildren will be able to spend for their needs. It's all well and good to say that we're for all of the above, but reality requires us to make choices—and to boil our ideals down to what really matters to us the most.

What mattered most to Liberal Dave was making sure that America was truly the Land of Opportunity, a nation whose prosperity would allow even the poorest among us could enjoy basic material comforts, have access to affordable health care, get a proper education, and have a real shot at realizing the American Dream.

And he wanted oppressed people everywhere to enjoy the freedoms and opportunities he enjoyed as an American.

Both liberals and conservatives have policies that are intended to achieve Liberal Dave's basic ideals. Liberal policies rely more upon the government; conservatives place more faith in free markets and individual choice. Even liberals in America acknowledge that the free market is the engine of our economic system. And well they should: no system matches the productive power of capitalism, which has lifted more people out of poverty than any other. The problem with liberal policies is that they take the prosperity generated by capitalism for granted; liberals believe that government micromanagement can achieve "fair" outcomes without undermining capitalism's ability to generate that prosperity. But government micromanagement, which is performed by Politicrats who are no match for the dispassionate wisdom of the market, inevitably harms the goose that lays the golden egg. Liberals have endless faith in the ability of smart people to significantly improve upon the outcomes of the market; conservatives are smart enough to know that no one is that smart. Conservatives are also smart enough to know that catastrophic economic events such as the 2008 housing crisis are generally caused not by unbridled capitalism, but by unbridled meddling with capitalism by Politicrats.

Conservatives, with their faith in the market, understand that the best way to empower the poor is to ensure that they have choice so they can act as consumers. Whether they're "shopping" for a good education for their children or affordable health care for the entire family, people are better off with a multitude of providers competing to satisfy their needs—as the people themselves define those needs. That is much better than having the Politicrats decide what people's needs are and how to satisfy them. Conservatives also realize that Politicrats cannot wave a magic wand and eliminate economic tradeoffs. When Politicrats propose to give us things that we want, such as environmental protection, conservatives ask how much that would cost in terms of other things that we want, such as jobs for those who need them the most. When Politicrats propose massive spending that will supposedly improve our well being, conservatives ask how the resulting debt will affect the well being of our children and grandchildren.

Conservatives also have a strong belief in the rule of law. They are more likely than liberals to be offended by sanctuary city policies, and are more likely than liberals to be offended by the affront to our sovereignty inherent in illegal immigration. But they also are offended by the exploitation of illegal immigrants—and realize that the only way to stop that exploitation is to stop illegal immigration itself.

Both conservatives and liberals are appalled by the way that some people are treated in the world on account of their race, nationality, religion or gender. But conservatives, being less restrained than liberals by notions of multiculturalism, are more likely to insist that supposedly "Western" values are really universal values that should be invoked to defend the safety and dignity of every human being.

I've noticed over the years that conservatives are more focused on what they're for and liberals are more focused on who they're for. A person is likely to define himself as a conservative, for example, because he stands for the free market, liberty, limited government, and strong national defense. A person is likely to define himself as a liberal, on the other hand, because he's for the middle class, the poor, working people, women, minorities, etc.

If we could somehow get everyone to focus on what they're for, rather than who they're for, our society would be less divided, more fair, and less susceptible to political pandering (and the overspending and accumulation of government power that pandering inevitably leads to). Yeah, I know I'm dreaming, and my purpose here is not to make that value judgment. My purpose is to point out that the different ways that conservatives and liberals approach politics provides an opportunity to find common ground. Because, as I have tried to demonstrate in the preceding chapters, *what* conservatives are for happens to be the best way to protect *who* liberals are for (and the rest of us as well).

For example, we need to remember—as many have said—that the best anti-poverty program is a job. We need to recognize, though, that when government usurps more and more of the private sector's role in creating jobs, it adds to the already crushing debt burden that we're passing on to our children and grandchildren. We have no choice but to get control over that debt burden and reign in the growth of government—otherwise, government will be unable to support the neediest in our society in future generations. We need to recognize that government revenues grow naturally with a healthy and growing private sector, and that it is counterproductive to try to raise revenues by overburdening a stagnant and struggling private sector. That means that we need to get the Politicrats off the private sector's back so that businesses can create enough jobs for the people who desperately need them. That means that we have to avoid the excessive taxation and regulation that makes it too costly for the private sector to make the investments that create jobs. We have to understand the dynamics that enable the private sector to create prosperity and squeeze out inefficiency, so that we can apply those dynamics to help the segments of our society that need them the most. That means that we need to empower poor people (and the rest of us) with consumer choice—in education, in health care— rather than weakening and infantilizing them with government dependence.

This book is designed to suggest a pathway for folks who are idealistic, but who realize that caring means caring about results— it's not enough to have good intentions. I believe that ConservaDave's idealism is stronger than Liberal Dave's—stronger because it is founded in realism, an understanding of how the world *is* which is crucial to charting a path to what it could be.

In describing the "Left-Hearted, Right-Minded" approach to various issues, "Left-Hearted" is of course meant to cast liberal intentions in a positive light. I do not mean to imply, though, that all of the good hearts reside on the left. Liberal Dave may have thought that; ConservaDave knows better. There are plenty of good hearts—and bad hearts—at both ends of the political spectrum. What the title means to suggest, rather, is that a liberal can move rightward, as I have done, without changing his heart. I was once left-hearted and left-minded, and I'm now left-hearted and right-minded: I changed my mind without changing my heart.

This book has dealt with many issues, but we have not discussed social issues such as abortion and gay marriage. For those issues, the religious beliefs—or lack thereof—of people on opposite sides add layers of complexity to the "Left-Hearted, Right-Minded" analysis that would warrant another book.

I would note that ConservaDave's conservatism fits equally well with social liberalism as it does with social conservatism. There is no rule, for example, that says that anyone who favors gay marriage must also favor fiscal profligacy, turning the economy over to the Politicrats or trapping poor children in failing public schools. People should reflect upon their own values and beliefs and mix and match their politics as necessary to suit themselves. It seems that our political process is now geared to pressure candidates to be "pure" conservatives or liberals. But here's something on which Liberal Dave and ConservaDave wholeheartedly agree: Never sacrifice your individuality in the service of an ideology. That's un-American. In fact, it's a totalitarian mindset. If you are genuinely a "pure" conservative or a "pure" liberal, that's fine—but pursuing purity for purity's sake will ultimately require you to override your best judgment, which is never a good thing.

For liberals that have gotten this far into the book (hang in there, it's almost over!), there is no need for you to agree with ConservaDave on every issue. I'm not asking you to reject one party line in favor of another. What I hope that all readers of this book will do, liberal or conservative, is to go through the exercise that I went through: test your assumptions, question your beliefs. After having done that, you may end up in exactly the same point in the ideological spectrum that you were when you started. Or, like me, you may end up somewhere completely different. Either result is fine. And either way, you will be a more thoughtful citizen for having undertaken the exercise.

People who go through the exercise will be less likely to automatically demonize those with whom they disagree. Certain people deserve to be demonized—this book has discussed some of them—but that judgment should arise from thoughtful analysis rather than reflex. Reflexive demonization usually occurs out of ignorance. It's easier to jump to the conclusion that someone who disagrees with you is a bad person if you've never taken the time to understand the intellectual basis for their argument. Once you've taken the time to understand the other view and have found at least some merit in it, you no longer have an excuse to demonize someone simply for holding that view.

Demonizing others just because they disagree with you can become a harmful habit that erodes your decency. Liberal Dave should have been revolted when his college friend reacted to President Reagan's shooting by writing "I hope he dies." Liberal Dave wasn't able to feel that revulsion, however. He had been conditioned to believe that Reagan was a bad person for having conservative views, and that conditioning interfered with the functioning of his normal humane instincts.

If you do go through the exercise of testing your assumptions and questioning your beliefs, you may end up as a predictable, straight-down-the-line ideologue—but most likely you will not. Your individual idiosyncrasies are likely to shine through in unexpected places. As noted in the first chapter, ConservaDave opposes the death penalty. It's not because murderers don't deserve to die—they do.   But ConservaDave's healthy awareness of government's fallibility makes him unwilling to entrust the state with that power. He has heard more stories than he can count of people who spent years—sometimes decades—in prison for crimes they didn't commit. The death penalty presents too great of a risk of the state killing innocent people, which is the most disgusting outcome imaginable. ConservaDave is thus satisfied to just lock 'em up and throw away the key. Or maybe we should actually hold onto the key, just in case the state messed up.

ConservaDave is also a compassionate vegetarian. This is the result of having been corrupted by his Indian Hindu wife, who has been a compassionate vegetarian since birth. He had never given a thought to the moral issues involved in eating meat, until his girlfriend (who would later be demoted to his wife) posed the following question to him: "If you can get a proper diet without taking animal life, what is the justification for eating meat?" ConservaDave thought for a while. "Because it tastes good" was the first answer that came to mind, but upon reflection, that sounded like a pretty lame justification for taking the life of a sentient being. The old "protein" argument didn't really hold up to scientific scrutiny, and ConservaDave knew it. Thus stumped, ConservaDave no longer felt comfortable eating meat. Thus is the danger of being open to new ideas. But as a good conservative, ConservaDave has not attempted to get the government to stop *you* from eating meat; he has just made the personal choice to stop eating meat himself.

Now granted, not many conservatives are vegetarians. But is there any reason that vegetarianism is incompatible with conservatism?   There isn't.   If we're too willing to accept prepackaged, group-think mindsets, we'll all gravitate to our respective opposing corners and associate only with people who are just like us. Some people like it that way. But then what's the point of having a vibrant, diverse society if you're only going to experience a small part of it? Liberals are good at celebrating the racial and ethnic diversity that enriches our society—but diversity of thought is even more important than diversity of skin color. So long live the vegetarian conservatives (I mean that literally, at least in my case) and the religiously devout liberals. People whose political thinking defies stereotypes are less likely to be bound by rigid orthodoxy. They are more likely to have the creativity to find common ground with those who think differently.

And speaking of defying stereotypes, there's a special place in my heart for African Americans and women who have the guts to openly proclaim their conservatism. I say "guts" because these folks are singled out for the most hateful kind of vitriol from many on the left. This vitriol includes, in many cases, slurs that these same leftists would consider racist or sexist had they been hurled at blacks or women who thought the way they're "supposed to" think. The people who spew these slurs somehow think that they're the enlightened ones—even as they suggest by implication that members of an entire race or gender all have to think alike. I am particularly amused by leftist white males who presume to be the arbiters of what African Americans and women are supposed to think. These people seem to believe that the crime of thinking differently is punishable by the forfeiture of one's dignity. But do any of us believe that being born black or female should limit what you're allowed to *achieve* in life? Then why should it limit what you're allowed to *think*?

Perhaps finding common ground comes naturally for one who is both Samoan and Jewish and fully embraces both lines of his heritage. My comfort with dualities might explain why I continue to embrace the Liberal Dave in me, even though I have long since stopped taking policy advice from him. But hopefully, one does not have to be a Jewish Samoan liberal-turned-conservative to adopt the Left-Hearted, Right-Minded approach to the world.

The past several chapters have outlined ConservaDave's brand of conservatism. It is a fairly typical brand of conservatism, although you wouldn't know that from the way the conservative movement is typically described in the media. This is not the politics of the angry old white racists and religious fanatics who populate the media stereotypes. It is the politics of people with open minds and open hearts who want to improve their community, their nation and their world. It is a hopeful, youthful, idealistic and optimistic conservatism that can give meaning to the idealism of "young people of all ages" for generations to come.

NOTES

1 Liberal Dave

[1] From the song "Ohio," written by Neil Young.
[2] From the song "Chicago," written by Graham Nash.
[3] From the song "The Times They Are a-Changin'," written by Bob Dylan.
[4] See, for example, Rothman, Lichter and Nevitte, "Politics and Professional Advancement Among College Faculty," published in *The Forum,* volume 3, issue 1 (2005). The study, based upon 1999 data, found that 72 percent of college professors described themselves as "left" or "liberal" (compared with 18 percent of the general public) and 15 percent described themselves as "right" or "conservative" (compared with 37 percent of the general public).
[5] From the song "Imagine," written by John Lennon.

2 The Birth of ConservaDave, Part I

[6] Gottemoeller, "Looking Back: The Intermediate-Range Nuclear Forces Treaty," *Arms Control Today* (June 2007). For other accounts of these events, see, for example, Wittner, "Reagan and Nuclear Disarmament," *Boston Review* (April-May 2000), which is presented from a liberal perspective, and Smith, "The Legacy of Ronald Reagan—Peace," Newsmax.com (June 10, 2004), which is presented from a conservative perspective.
[7] That is, ultimately, what happened, as recounted in the Gottemoeller article cited above.
[8] President Reagan's address to a meeting of the National Association of Evangelicals, Orlando, Florida, March 8, 1983.
[9] Lewis, "Onward Christian Soliders," *New York Times*, March 10, 1983.
[10] Wicker, "In the Nation: Two Dangerous Doctrines," *New York Times*, March 15, 1983.
[11] Peterson, "Reagan's Use of Moral Language to Explain Policies Draws Fire," *Washington Post*, March 23, 1983. The foregoing quotes reacting to Reagan's "Evil Empire" speech are samples from a compilation of reaction quotes on Newt Gingrich's website at
http://newt.org/tabid/102/articleType/ArticleView/articleId/3234/Default.aspx.
[12] "The View from the Gulag," *Weekly Standard*, June 21, 2004.
[13] Talbott, *The Russians and Reagan* (New York, Vintage, 1984).
[14] The online *Museum of Communism*,
http://economics.gmu.edu/bcaplan/museum/faqframe.htm, contains a wealth of information documenting the atrocities of the Soviet Union and other communist regimes.
[15] This information is from the online *Museum of Communism*,
http://economics.gmu.edu/bcaplan/museum/faqframe.htm.
[16] From the song "Love and Affection," written by Joan Armatrading.

3 The Birth of ConservaDave, Part II

[17] I again stress that I'm recreating the gist of Hogan's remarks to the best of my recollection; these are not exact quotes.

[18] See, for example, Rector and Fagan, "How Welfare Harms Kids," Heritage Foundation Backgrounder No. 1084, June 5, 1996.

[19] See, for example, "Education is the Means of Social Mobility," Rediff News, May 30, 2006 (http://in.rediff.com/news/2006/may/30spec.htm).

[20] "Education is the Means of Social Mobility," Rediff News, May 30, 2006 (http://in.rediff.com/news/2006/may/30spec.htm).

[21] Brooks, *Who Really Cares: The Surprising Truth About Compassionate Conservatism*. See also Gose, "Charity's Political Divide: Republicans Give a Bigger Share of Their Incomes to Charity, Says a Prominent Economist," *The Chronicle of Philanthropy*, November 23, 2006.

4 Left-Hearted, Right-Minded

[22] McCormack, "President Bush 'Look-Alike' a Cross Between Satan and Hitler?" *NewsBusters*, January 13, 2006 (http://newsbusters.org/node/3586).

[23] Roesgen's tour de force of objective journalism is on display on YouTube at http://www.youtube.com/watch?v=wCA-3q6t57Q.

[24] Santelli's rant is captured on YouTube at http://www.youtube.com/watch?v=bEZB4taSEoA.

[25] See http://www.urbandictionary.com/define.php?term=teabagger.

[26] This exchange can be found on YouTube at http://www.youtube.com/watch?v=I64Ed5iLu4M.

[27] This report can be found on YouTube at http://www.youtube.com/watch?v=ELy61zkZHO0.

[28] Congressional Budget Office, *Estimated Impact of the American Recovery and Reinvestment Act on Employment and Economic Output from January 2011 Through March 2011*, May 2011.

[29] "The Era of Big Government is Over," CNN transcript of President Clinton's radio address, January 27, 1996 (http://www.cnn.com/US/9601/budget/01-27/clinton_radio/).

[30] DeFeo, "National Debt by President: LBJ to Obama," *The Street*, January 4, 2011 (http://www.thestreet.com/story/10959884/1/national-debt-a-look-at-presidents-tabs.html).

[31] Dickerson, "Confessions of a White House Insider," *Time Magazine World*, January 10, 2004 (http://www.time.com/time/magazine/article/0,9171,574809,00.html).

[32] See footnote 30.

[33] Milbank, "Bush Administration Announces $159 Billion Deficit for Year 2002," *The Washington Post*, as reproduced in *The Tech*, October 25, 2002 (http://tech.mit.edu/V122/N50/spending-50.50w.html).

[34] Montgomery, "Federal Budget Deficit to Exceed $1.4 Trillion in 2010 and 2011," *The Washington Post*, July 24, 2010 (http://www.washingtonpost.com/wp-dyn/content/article/2010/07/23/AR2010072304101.html).

[35] "National Debt Hits $15 Trillion as Congress Strains to Cut $1.2 Trillion from Deficits," *FoxNews.com*, November 16, 2011 (http://www.foxnews.com/politics/2011/11/16/national-debt-hits-15t-as-congress-strains-to-cut-12t/).

[36] "Gross Domestic Product 2010," *WorldBank.org* (http://siteresources.worldbank.org/DATASTATISTICS/Resources/GDP.pdf).

[37] Seib, "As Budget Battle Rages On, A Quiet Cancer Grows," *The Wall Street Journal*, March 8, 2011 (http://online.wsj.com/article/SB10001424052748703883504576186163767307644.html).

[38] U.S. Department of the Treasury, Bureau of the Public Debt, "Monthly Statement of the Public Debt of the United States," January 31, 2011 (http://www.treasurydirect.gov/govt/reports/pd/mspd/2011/opds012011.pdf). Publicly held debt is added to intergovernmental debt (primarily borrowings from the Social Security Trust Fund to finance general governmental operations) to get total federal debt. Foreigners own about 32 percent of total federal debt.

[39] Department of the Treasury/Federal Reserve Board, "Major Foreign Holders of Treasury Securities," October 18, 2011 (http://www.treasury.gov/resource-center/data-chart-center/tic/Documents/mfh.txt).

[40] Goldfarb, "S&P Downgrades U.S. Credit Rating for First Time," *The Washington Post*, August 5, 2011 (http://www.washingtonpost.com/business/economy/sandp-considering-first-downgrade-of-us-credit-rating/2011/08/05/gIQAqKeIxI_story.html).

[41] Eichengreen, "Why the Dollar's Reign is Near an End," *The Wall Street Journal*, March 2, 2011 (http://online.wsj.com/article/SB10001424052748703313304576132170181013248.html).

[42] New, "Could the U.S. Print its Way Out of the Debt Crisis?" *DailyFinance* July 28, 2011 (http://www.dailyfinance.com/2011/07/28/could-the-u-s-print-its-way-out-of-the-debt-crisis/).

[43] Seib, "As Budget Battle Rages On, A Quiet Cancer Grows," *The Wall Street Journal*, March 8, 2011 (http://online.wsj.com/article/SB10001424052748703883504576186163767307644.html).

[44] "Where the Tax Money Is," *The Wall Street Journal*, April 17, 2011 (http://online.wsj.com/article/SB10001424052748704621304576267113524583554.html).

[45] U.S. Federal Spending, Fiscal Year 2010, Wikipedia (http://upload.wikimedia.org/wikipedia/en/7/7a/U.S._Federal_Spending_-_FY_2007.png).

[46] Becatoros, "Greece: Riots as Austerity Steps Get 1st Approval," *Associated Press*, October 19, 2011 (http://news.yahoo.com/greece-riots-austerity-steps-1st-approval-195223157.html).
[47] de Rugy, "The Real S&P Warning: A $4 Trillion Deal or a Downgrade," *National Review Online*, July 19, 2011 (http://www.nationalreview.com/corner/272202/real-sp-warning-4-trillion-deal-or-downgrade-veronique-de-rugy).

5 Liberal Dave vs. ConservaDave: Soon to be a Major Motion Picture

[48] "Who Pays Income Taxes and How Much?" *National Taxpayers Union* (http://ntu.org/tax-basics/who-pays-income-taxes.html).
[49] Sahadi, "47% Will Pay No Federal Income Tax," *CNNMoney*, October 3, 2009 (http://money.cnn.com/2009/09/30/pf/taxes/who_pays_taxes/index.htm).
[50] Will, "Conservatives More Liberal Givers," *RealClearPolitics*, March 27, 2008 (http://www.realclearpolitics.com/articles/2008/03/conservatives_more_liberal_giv.html).
[51] Meyers and Ruddy, "Ex-President Clinton to NewsMax: Raising Taxes Won't Work," *NewsMax.com*, September 20, 2011 (http://www.newsmax.com/Headline/bill-clinton-obama-taxes/2011/09/20/id/411720).
[52] "Flashback: Obama Says 'You Don't Raise Taxes in a Recession,'" *Breitbart.TV* (http://www.breitbart.tv/flashback-obama-says-you-dont-raise-taxes-in-a-recession/).
[53] See, e.g., Sherrill, "Speaking Up for American Capitalism," *The Wall Street Journal*, July 15, 2010 (http://online.wsj.com/article/SB10001424052748704518904575365161631063340.html).
[54] Singleton, "The Critics Are Wrong: Global Capitalism is a 250-Year Success Story," *The Telegraph*, December 9, 2009 (http://blogs.telegraph.co.uk/news/alexsingleton/5929357/The_critics_are_wrong_global_capitalism_is_a_250year_success_story/).

6 Education: "The Great Civil Rights Issue of Our Time"

[55] "Amy Carter Starts Public School Today," *The Ocala StarBanner* (from AP), January 24, 1977 (http://news.google.com/newspapers?nid=1356&dat=19770124&id=ZMswAAAAIBAJ&sjid=oQUEAAAAIBAJ&pg=5970,5110280).
[56] St. Clair, "American Girls: For Obama's Daughters, White House Life Isn't Going to be Normal," *Chicago Tribune*, November 7, 2008 (http://www.chicagotribune.com/news/local/chi-first-family-07-nov07,0,6338748.story).
[57] De Witt, "THE TRANSITION: Chelsea's School; Public or Private?" *The New York Times*, December 13, 1992

(http://query.nytimes.com/gst/fullpage.html?res=9F0CE2DD1538F930A25751C1
A964958260).

[58] These student profiles are summarized from information available on the
Waiting for Superman web site (http://www.waitingforsuperman.com).

[59] Fleischman, H.L., Hopstock, P.J., Pelczar, M.P., and Shelley, B.E. (2010).
*Highlights From PISA 2009: Performance of U.S. 15-Year-Old Students in
Reading, Mathematics, and Science Literacy in an International Context* (NCES
2011-004). U.S. Department of Education, National Center for Education
Statistics. Washington, DC: U.S. Government Printing Office
(http://nces.ed.gov/pubs2011/2011004.pdf).

[60] "OECD Calls for Broader Access to Post-School Education and Training,"
Organization of Economic Cooperation and Development, September 13, 2005
(http://www.oecd.org/document/34/0,2340,en_2649_201185_35341645_1_1_1_1,
00.html).

[61] Keating and Haynes, "Can D.C. Schools be Fixed?" *The Washington Post*, June
10, 2007 (http://www.washingtonpost.com/wp-
dyn/content/article/2007/06/09/AR2007060901415.html?hpid=topnews).

[62] Fertig, "Some Rubber Room Teachers Say They're Still Waiting," *WNYC News*,
September 22, 2010 (http://www.wnyc.org/articles/wnyc-news/2010/sep/22/some-
rubber-room-teachers-say-theyre-still-waiting/).

[63] Katie Couric interview with Davis Guggenheim, *CBS News @katiecouric*,
September 23, 2010 (http://www.cbsnews.com/video/watch/?id=6895090n).

[64] Anderson, "Waiting for Superman," *Variety*, January 23, 2010.

[65] Klein, "The Failure of American Schools," *Atlantic Magazine*, June 2011
(http://www.theatlantic.com/magazine/archive/2011/06/the-failure-of-american-
schools/8497/1/#).

[66] Di Carlo and Quintero, "Quote, Unquote," *Shanker Blog: The Voice of the
Albert Shanker Institute*, May 13, 2011 (http://shankerblog.org/?p=2562).

[67] Endorsements are listed on the Save Our Schools website
(http://www.saveourschoolsmarch.org/about/endorsers/#ed_organizations_leaders)
.

[68] "What We Saw at the Save Our Schools Rally in Washington, D.C." *Reason TV*,
July 30, 2011 (http://www.youtube.com/watch?v=TJ7icVvDK9I).

[69] "Michael Moore: Matt Damon for President," *HuffPost Entertainment*, August
9, 2011 (http://www.huffingtonpost.com/2011/08/09/michael-moore-matt-damon-
president_n_922740.html).

[70] "OECD Calls for Broader Access to Post-School Education and Training,"
Organization of Economic Cooperation and Development, September 13, 2005
(http://www.oecd.org/document/34/0,2340,en_2649_201185_35341645_1_1_1_1,
00.html).

[71] Coulson, "The Effect of Teachers Unions on American Education," *CATO
Journal*, 2010 (http://www.cato.org/pubs/journal/cj30n1/cj30n1-8.pdf).

[72] See footnote 70.

[73] Gillespie, "The Father of Modern School Reform," *Reason.com*, December
2005 (http://reason.com/archives/2005/12/01/the-father-of-modern-school-re).

[74] Dalmia, "Teachers Go to the Matt," *The Daily*, August 11, 2011 (http://www.thedaily.com/page/2011/08/11/081111-opinions-column-damon-dalmia-1-3/).

7 Nursing Our Health Care System Back to Health

[75] "National Health Insurance—A Brief History of Reform Efforts in the U.S.," The Henry J. Kaiser Family Foundation, March 2009 (http://www.kff.org/healthreform/upload/7871.pdf).
[76] Pear and Herzenhorn, "Obama Hails Vote on Health Care as Answering 'the Call of History,'" *The New York Times*, March 21, 2010 (http://www.nytimes.com/2010/03/22/health/policy/22health.html?pagewanted=all).
[77] Attkisson, "Health Care Passage Plan Unconstitutional?" *CBSNews.com*, March 18, 2010 (http://www.cbsnews.com/stories/2010/03/17/eveningnews/main6308849.shtml).
[78] Both President Obama and Rep. Clyburn are quoted from Pear and Herzenhorn, "Obama Hails Vote on Health Care as Answering 'the Call of History,'" *The New York Times*, March 21, 2010 (http://www.nytimes.com/2010/03/22/health/policy/22health.html?pagewanted=all).
[79] "'A Big F—ing Deal': Biden's Health Care Reform F-Bomb on Live TV," *HuffPost Politics*, March 23, 2010 (http://www.huffingtonpost.com/2010/03/23/a-big-fucking-deal-bidens_n_509927.html).
[80] DeNavas-Walt, Proctor and Smith, "Income, Poverty, and Health Insurance Coverage in the United States: 2009," U.S. Census Bureau, September 2009 (http://www.census.gov/prod/2010pubs/p60-238.pdf).
[81] "World Health Statistics 2009," World Health Organization, May 2009 (http://www.who.int/whosis/whostat/EN_WHS09_Table7.pdf).
[82] Turner, Capretta, Miller and Moffit, *Why Obamacare is Wrong for America* (Broadside, 2011), p. 9.
[83] Freddoso, "Pelosi on Health Care: 'We Have to Pass the Bill So You Can Find Out What is in It,'" *The Examiner*, March 9, 2010 (http://washingtonexaminer.com/blogs/beltway-confidential/pelosi-health-care-039we-have-pass-bill-so-you-can-find-out-what-it039).
[84] See, for example, Jackson and Nolan, "Health Care Reform Bill Summary: A Look at What's in the Bill," *CBSNews.com*, March 21, 2010 (http://www.cbsnews.com/8301-503544_162-20000846-503544.html); Grier, "Health Care Reform Bill 101: What the Bill Means to You," *The Christian Science Monitor*, March 22, 2010 (http://www.csmonitor.com/USA/Politics/2010/0322/Health-care-reform-bill-101-what-the-bill-means-to-you); and Tanner, "Bad Medicine: A Guide to the Real Costs and Consequences of the New Health Care Law," CATO Institute, 2011 (http://www.cato.org/pubs/wtpapers/BadMedicineWP.pdf).

[85] Tanner, "Bad Medicine: A Guide to the Real Costs and Consequences of the New Health Care Law," CATO Institute, 2011 (http://www.cato.org/pubs/wtpapers/BadMedicineWP.pdf).

[86] One exception to this rule is the Medicare Part D prescription-drug program, enacted in 2003, which relies heavily on price competition among many participating insurance plans. Fiegl, "Medicare Spends 50% Less on Part D Drugs Than Initially Estimated," *amendnews.com (American Medical News)*, August 1, 2011 (http://www.ama-assn.org/amednews/2011/08/01/gvsc0801.htm).

[87] "U.S. Health Plans Have a History of Cost Overruns," *The Washington Times*, November 18, 2009 (http://www.washingtontimes.com/news/2009/nov/18/health-programs-have-history-of-cost-overruns/print/).

[88] "U.S. Health Plans Have a History of Cost Overruns," *The Washington Times*, November 18, 2009 (http://www.washingtontimes.com/news/2009/nov/18/health-programs-have-history-of-cost-overruns/print/).

[89] Tanner, "Bad Medicine: A Guide to the Real Costs and Consequences of the New Health Care Law," CATO Institute, 2011 (http://www.cato.org/pubs/wtpapers/BadMedicineWP.pdf).

[90] Chaddock, "Piece by Piece, Will Obama's Health-Care Reform Law Be Dismantled?" *The Christian Science Monitor*, November 2, 2011 (http://news.yahoo.com/piece-piece-obamas-health-care-reform-law-dismantled-170150639.html).

[91] Turner, Capretta, Miller and Moffit, *Why Obamacare is Wrong for America* (Broadside, 2011).

[92] Turner, Capretta, Miller and Moffit, *Why Obamacare is Wrong for America* (Broadside, 2011), p. 10, 22.

[93] Powers, "Nancy Pelosi on 1,800 Obamacare Waiver Recipients: Mostly Very Small Companies," *michellemalkin.com*, October 29, 2011 (http://michellemalkin.com/2011/10/29/pelosi-obamacare-waiver/).

[94] Levey, "U.S. Halts New Applications for Waivers on Health Coverage Rule," *Los Angeles Times*, June 18, 2011 (http://articles.latimes.com/2011/jun/18/business/la-fi-healthcare-waivers-20110618).

[95] Wolf, "Obamacare Waiver Corruption Must Stop," *The Washington Times*, May 20, 2011 (http://www.washingtontimes.com/news/2011/may/20/obamacare-waiver-corruption-must-stop/).

[96] Powers, "Nancy Pelosi on 1,800 Obamacare Waiver Recipients: Mostly Very Small Companies," *michellemalkin.com*, October 29, 2011 (http://michellemalkin.com/2011/10/29/pelosi-obamacare-waiver/); Demirjian, "ENTIRE State of Nevada Scores Obamacare Waiver," *The Policy Racket*, as published in *FoxNation*, May 16, 2011 (http://nation.foxnews.com/obamacare/2011/05/18/entire-state-nevada-scores-obamacare-waiver).

[97] Sherk, "Recovery Stalled After Obamacare Passed," The Heritage Foundation, July 19, 2011 (http://www.heritage.org/research/reports/2011/07/economic-recovery-stalled-after-obamacare-passed).

[98] Tanner, "Bad Medicine: A Guide to the Real Costs and Consequences of the New Health Care Law," CATO Institute, 2011, p. 9, footnotes omitted (http://www.cato.org/pubs/wtpapers/BadMedicineWP.pdf).

[99] Haberkorn, "Insurers Ending Child-Only Policies," *Politico*, September 21, 2010 (http://www.politico.com/news/stories/0910/42443.html).

[100] Tanner, "Bad Medicine: A Guide to the Real Costs and Consequences of the New Health Care Law," CATO Institute, 2011, p. 9, footnotes omitted (http://www.cato.org/pubs/wtpapers/BadMedicineWP.pdf).

[101] Andrews, "Graduates May See Coverage Gap After All," *The New York Times*, May 31, 2010 (http://www.nytimes.com/2010/06/01/health/01landscape.html).

[102] Cover, "Obamacare Has Increased Cost of Health Insurance, Says Kaiser Foundation," *cnsnews.com*, September 27, 2011 (http://cnsnews.com/news/article/obamacare-has-increased-cost-health-insurance-says-kaiser-foundation).

[103] This scenario was outlined in a different form in Levy, "Taking Government to a Whole New Level," *CATO Policy Report*, March/April 2010 (http://www.cato.org/pubs/policy_report/v32n2/cpr32n2-2.html).

[104] "Proposed Retirement Age Change Prompts Riots in France," *Associated Press*, as published in the *Chicago Sun-Times*, October 20, 2010 (http://www.suntimes.com/business/2244613-420/story.html).

[105] Turner, Capretta, Miller and Moffit, *Why Obamacare is Wrong for America* (Broadside, 2011).

[106] Sahadi, "Family Health Costs Jump 5%," *CNNMoney*, September 15, 2009 (http://money.cnn.com/2009/09/15/news/economy/health_insurance_costs/index.htm).

[107] Turner, Capretta, Miller and Moffit, *Why Obamacare is Wrong for America*, p. 198 (Broadside, 2011).

[108] Capretta and Miller, "How to Cover Pre-existing Conditions," *National Affairs*, Summer 2010 (http://www.nationalaffairs.com/publications/detail/how-to-cover-pre-existing-conditions).

[109] Lott, "As Obama Pushes National Health Care, Most Americans Already Happy with Coverage," *FoxNews.com*, June 24, 2009 (http://www.foxnews.com/politics/2009/06/24/obama-pushes-national-health-care-americans-happy-coverage/).

8 A Nation of Immigrants

[110] Bowe, *Nobodies: Modern Slave Labor and the Dark Side of the New Global Economy* (Random House 2007). The quotations from the book are from pages 3 through 13.

[111] "Annihilation of the Jews in the Districts of Grajewo and Lomza in July 1941," *Radzilow*, Province, Jewish Historical Commission, Bialystok, 14 May 1946 (http://www.radzilow.com/districtpogroms.htm).

[112] Shadia, "Costa Mesa Declares Itself a 'Rule of Law' Community," *Los Angeles Times*, May 20, 2010 (http://articles.latimes.com/2010/may/20/local/la-me-0520-costa-mesa-immigration-20100520).

[113] "Hysterical Nativism," *The Economist*, April 22, 2010 (http://www.economist.com/node/15954262).

[114] See, for example, Wise, "Reflections on Racism and Reasonable Suspicion: Immigration, Arizona and Anti-Latino Bias," *TimWise*, May 12, 2010 (http://www.timwise.org/2010/05/reflections-on-racism-and-reasonable-suspicion-immigration-arizona-and-anti-latino-bias/).

[115] Zimmermann, "Obama Warns of Racial Profiling as a Result of Arizona Law on Immigration," *The Hill*, May 27, 2010 (http://thehill.com/blogs/blog-briefing-room/news/94711-obama-warns-of-racial-profiling-in-arizona).

[116] Hall, "Shep Smith Compares Arizona Immigration Law to 'Driving While Black' Law," *Mediaite*, April 27, 2010 (http://www.mediaite.com/tv/shep-smith-compares-arizona-immigration-law-to-driving-while-black-law/).

[117] Picket, "Ariz. Immigration Law Mirrors Federal Version But With State Enforcement," *The Washington Times*, April 26, 2010 (http://www.washingtontimes.com/weblogs/watercooler/2010/apr/26/ariz-immigration-law-mirrors-federal-version-state/).

[118] Percha, "Justice Department Sues Arizona for Immigration Law—But Does Not Make Charges of 'Discrimination,'" *ABC News*, July 6, 2010 (http://abcnews.go.com/blogs/politics/2010/07/justice-department-sues-arizona-for-immigration-law/).

[119] Harris and Schoenberg, "Alabama's Immigration Laws Are Unconstitutional, U.S. Tells Appeals Court," *Bloomberg*, November 15, 2011 (http://www.bloomberg.com/news/2011-11-15/alabama-immigration-laws-are-unconstitutional-u-s-tells-appeals-court.html).

[120] Chel, "Why the Border Fence is a Bad Idea," *Newsvine.com*, December 1, 2010 (http://merena29.newsvine.com/_news/2010/12/01/5560774-why-the-border-fence-is-a-bad-idea).

[121] Castaneda, "Immigration: Do Bad Fences Make Bad Neighbors?" *big think*, February 16, 2010 (http://bigthink.com/ideas/18673).

[122] This is a reference to a bill that was being considered by the Senate when Krauthammer wrote this column in 2007.

[123] Krauthammer, "We Agree on Border Security, Don't We?" *Real Clear Politics*, June 15, 2007 (http://www.realclearpolitics.com/articles/2007/06/we_agree_on_border_security_do.html).

[124] See, for example, Chavez, "We Shouldn't Militarize the U.S.-Mexico Border," *The Progressive*, March 23, 2009 (http://www.progressive.org/mag/mpleyva032309.html).

[125] Swarns, "Failed Amnesty Legislation of 1986 Haunts the Current Immigration Bills in Congress," *The New York Times*, May 23, 2006 (http://www.nytimes.com/2006/05/23/washington/23amnesty.html?pagewanted=al l).

9 Environmentalism: Separating Church from State

[126] Transcript of Speech by Van Jones, President, Ella Baker Center for Human Rights at Full Circle Fund's annual event, Forum 2007: You've Got the Power! November 14, 2007, San Francisco, CA (http://www.fullcirclefund.org/downloads/Forum2007_VJones_speechtranscript.pdf).

[127] Wilson and Franke-Ruta, "White House Advisor Van Jones Resigns Amid Controversy Over Past Activism," *The Washington Post*, September 6, 2009 (http://voices.washingtonpost.com/44/2009/09/06/van_jones_resigns.html).

[128] "Obama's Green Jobs Czar Van Jones: Republicans Are 'A**holes,'" *Real Clear Politics*, September 2, 2009 (http://www.realclearpolitics.com/video/2009/09/02/obamas_green_jobs_czar_van_jones_republicans_are_aholes.html).

[129] "Catch-up on the Solyndra Scandal," *iWatch News*, The Center for Public Integrity (http://www.iwatchnews.org/2011/09/20/6674/solyndra-timeline). The rest of the factual account of the Solyndra story in the text is also taken from this source, unless otherwise indicated.

[130] Leonnig and Stephens, "Solyndra: Energy Dept. Pushed Firm to Keep Layoffs Quite Until After Midterms," *The Washington Post*, November 15, 2011 (http://www.washingtonpost.com/politics/solyndra-department-of-energy-pushed-hard-for-company-not-to-announce-layoffs-until-after-2010-mid-term-elections/2011/11/15/gIQA2AriON_story.html).

[131] Saunders, "A Total Eclipse of Solyndra," *Townhall.com*, September 27, 2011 (http://townhall.com/columnists/debrajsaunders/2011/09/27/a_total_eclipse_of_solyndra/page/full/).

[132] "Obama Donor Discussed Solyndra Loan with White House, Emails Say," *Associated Press*, as published in *The Washington Post*, November 9, 2011 (http://www.washingtonpost.com/business/obama-donor-discussed-solyndra-loan-with-white-house/2011/11/09/gIQA6uys5M_story.html).

[133] Ransom, "Congress Likely to Cram Down Solyndra Billionaire," *Townhall.com*, September 16, 2011 (http://finance.townhall.com/columnists/johnransom/2011/09/16/congress_likely_to_cram_down_solyndra_billionaire/page/full/).

[134] "Solutions for America: Meeting America's Energy and Environmental Needs," *The Heritage Foundation*, August 17, 2010 (http://www.heritage.org/Research/Reports/2010/08/Meeting-America-s-Energy-and-Environmental-Needs).

[135] Wing, "Joe Machin Shoots Cap-and-Trade Bill with Rifle in New Ad," *HuffPost Politics*, October 11, 2011 (http://www.huffingtonpost.com/2010/10/11/joe-manchin-ad-dead-aim_n_758457.html).

[136] Furchtgott-Roth, "Don't Forget the Job Killing EPA, Mr. Obama," *RealClearMarkets*, September 8, 2011 (http://www.realclearmarkets.com/articles/2011/09/08/dont_forget_the_job_killing_epa_mr_obama_99240.html).

[137] Sheppard, "The Final Decision on the Keystone XL Pipeline is Coming Soon," *Mother Jones*, October 7, 2011 (http://motherjones.com/blue-marble/2011/10/keystone-xl-consideration-moves-final-stages).

[138] Loris, "Obama Delays Keystone Pipeline: Delays Jobs and Energy, Too," *The Foundry*, November 10, 2011 (http://blog.heritage.org/2011/11/10/obama-delays-keystone-pipeline-delays-jobs-and-energy-too/).

[139] Schor, "Canada-U.S. Oil Pipeline Poses Few Environmental Risks—State Dept.," *The New York Times*, August 26, 2011 (http://www.nytimes.com/gwire/2011/08/26/26greenwire-canada-us-oil-pipeline-poses-few-environmental-63932.html?pagewanted=all).

[140] Green, "Keystone Decision Exposes Obama's Energy Agenda," *The Daily Caller*, November 15, 2011 (http://dailycaller.com/2011/11/15/keystone-decision-exposes-obamas-energy-agenda/?utm_source=MadMimi&utm_medium=email&utm_content=TheDC+Morning&utm_campaign=The+DC+Morning+&utm_term=_0D_0AKenneth+Green_3A+Keystone+decision+exposes+Obama_27s+energy+agenda).

[141] Crichton, "Environmentalism as Religion," September 15, 2003, published in *Three Speeches by Michael Crichton* (Science & Public Policy Institute 2009) (http://scienceandpublicpolicy.org/images/stories/papers/commentaries/crichton_3.pdf).

[142] Goldberg, "Oil: The Real Green Fuel," *Townhall.com*, June 16, 2010 (http://townhall.com/columnists/jonahgoldberg/2010/06/16/oil_the_real_green_fuel/page/full/).

[143] Krauthammer, "Whose Blowout Is It, Anyway?" *Townhall.com*, May 28, 2010 (http://townhall.com/columnists/charleskrauthammer/2010/05/28/whose_blowout_is_it_anyway/page/full/).

[144] Makris, "Offshore Drillng is Safer Than Importing Oil on Tankers, Environmental Expert Says," *examiner.com*, May 4, 2010 (http://www.examiner.com/animal-policy-in-national/offshore-drilling-is-safer-than-importing-oil-on-tankers-says-environmental-expert).

10 America and the World: The Freedom Agenda and the War on Terror

[145] Second Inaugural Address of President George W. Bush, January 20, 2005, published at *Bartleby.com* (http://www.bartleby.com/124/pres67.html).

[146] Benjamin, "How Many Have Gone to War," *Salon.com*, April 12, 2005 (http://www.salon.com/2005/04/12/troops_numbers/).

[147] Walsh, "Boycott Row Hits Afghan Election Over Fraud Claims," *The Observer*, October 9, 2004 (http://www.guardian.co.uk/world/2004/oct/10/afghanistan.declanwalsh).

[148] Otterman, "Middle East: Islam and Democracy," *Council on Foreign Relations*, September 19, 2003 (http://www.cfr.org/religion-and-politics/middle-east-islam-democracy/p7708).

[149] Minas, "Egypt, Obama, Bush and the 'Freedom Agenda,'" *The Drum*, February 25, 2011 (http://www.abc.net.au/unleashed/44208.html).

[150] "Saddam's Iraq: Key Events/Iran-Iraq War, 1980-1988/Chemical Warfare, 1983-1988," *BBC News* (http://news.bbc.co.uk/2/shared/spl/hi/middle_east/02/iraq_events/html/chemical_warfare.stm).

[151] See Public Law 105-338, Iraq Liberation Act of 1998, U.S. Government Printing Office (http://www.gpo.gov/fdsys/pkg/PLAW-105publ338/content-detail.html).

[152] Saunders, "Bush Lied is a Big Lie," *RealClearPolitics*, March 22, 2007 (http://www.realclearpolitics.com/articles/2007/03/bush_lied_is_the_big_lie.html). Some critics of the decision to invade Iraq, such as former U.N. weapons inspector Hans Blix, argue that Bush, British Prime Minister Tony Blair and Australian Prime Minister John Howard should have given the weapons inspections more of a chance. See Blix, "Iraq 2003: What the Leaders Say, and What They Leave Out," *Inside Story*, March 23, 2011 (http://inside.org.au/iraq-2003-blix/). But it appears that the allies had little faith in an inspection process that had been interrupted by an absence of almost four years, and feared that the process would only be used by Saddam as a dilatory tactic.

[153] Krauthammer, "Three Cheers for the Bush Doctrine," *Time Magazine*, March 7, 2005 (http://www.time.com/time/magazine/article/0,9171,1034732,00.html).

[154] Varadarajan, "Iraq's Political Miracle," *The Daily Beast*, March 3, 2010 (http://www.thedailybeast.com/articles/2010/03/03/iraqs-political-miracle.html).

[155] "The Path of Protest" (an interactive timeline of the Arab Spring), *The Guardian* (http://www.guardian.co.uk/world/interactive/2011/mar/22/middle-east-protest-interactive-timeline).

[156] Shenker, "Mohamed ElBaradei Warns of 'Tunisia-Style Explosion' in Egypt," *The Guardian*, January 18, 2011 (http://www.guardian.co.uk/world/2011/jan/18/mohamed-elbaradei-tunisia-egypt).

[157] McGreal and Shenker, "Hosni Mubarak Resigns—And Egypt Celebrates a New Dawn," *The Guardian*, February 11, 2011 (http://www.guardian.co.uk/world/2011/feb/11/hosni-mubarak-resigns-egypt-cairo).

[158] "Muammar Gaddafi: How He Died," *BBC*, October 31, 2011 (http://www.bbc.co.uk/news/world-africa-15390980).

[159] "Does Condoleezza Rice Memoir Help or Hurt the Bush 43 Legacy?" Open Mike, Nov. 5-6, 2011, *The Arena, Politico* (http://www.politico.com/arena/archive/open-mike-nov-5-6-2011.html#1C7D84C1-A868-4EBD-BC41-A1D614F1908D).

[160] "Freedom in the World 2011 Survey Release," *Freedom House*, January 13, 2011 (http://www.freedomhouse.org/template.cfm?page=594).

[161] Noe and Raad, "Islamist Win in Tunisia Sparks Worry About Egypt: Noe & Raad," *Bloomberg.com*, October 31, 2011 (http://www.bloomberg.com/news/2011-10-31/islamist-win-in-tunisia-sparks-worry-about-egypt-noe-raad.html).

[162] Rozen, "Egypt's Islamists Win Big in Parliament Polls, In Setback for Liberal Activists," *The Envoy*, December 1, 2011 (http://news.yahoo.com/blogs/envoy/egypt-islamists-win-big-parliament-polls-setback-liberal-160235763.html#more-5823).

[163] Pipes, "A Democratic Islam?" *Jerusalem Post*, April 17, 2008 (http://www.danielpipes.org/5517/a-democratic-islam).

[164] Noe and Raad, "Islamist Win in Tunisia Sparks Worry About Egypt: Noe & Raad," *Bloomberg.com*, October 31, 2011 (http://www.bloomberg.com/news/2011-10-31/islamist-win-in-tunisia-sparks-worry-about-egypt-noe-raad.html).

[165] Pipes, "A Democratic Islam?" *Jerusalem Post*, April 17, 2008 (http://www.danielpipes.org/5517/a-democratic-islam).

[166] Bajoria, "Egypt's Muslim Brotherhood," *Council on Foreign Relations*, February 3, 2011 (http://www.cfr.org/africa/egypts-muslim-brotherhood/p23991).

[167] Darwish, "Impossible Family Dynamics of Islam," *FrontPageMag.com*, January 29, 2003 (http://archive.frontpagemag.com/readArticle.aspx?ARTID=20079).

[168] "The Taliban's War Against Women," Bureau of Democracy, Human Rights and Labor, U.S. Department of State, November 17, 2001 (http://www.state.gov/g/drl/rls/6185.htm).

[169] "Restrictions on Women in Saudi Arabia," *The Telegraph*, November 24, 2011 (http://www.telegraph.co.uk/news/worldnews/middleeast/saudiarabia/8529945/Restrictions-on-women-in-Saudi-Arabia.html).

[170] Media, "Islam and Female Genital Mutilation," *EuropeNews*, June 18, 2009 (http://europenews.dk/en/node/24127); "Violence Against Women Information," Amnesty International (http://www.amnestyusa.org/our-work/issues/women-s-rights/violence-against-women/violence-against-women-information?id=1108439).

[171] "Afghan President Pardons Woman Serving 12 Years Time for Being Rape Victim," *Associated Press*, as published in *The Washington Post*, December 1, 2011 (http://www.washingtonpost.com/world/asia-pacific/afghan-president-pardons-woman-serving-12-years-time-for-being-rape-victim/2011/12/01/gIQAZUL7GO_story.html).

[172] Jacoby, "Multiculturalism and its Discontents," *Big Questions Online*, August 19, 2010 (http://www.bigquestionsonline.com/columns/susan-jacoby/multiculturalism-and-its-discontents).

[173] Tucker, "True Unbeliever," *The Washington Post*, March 7, 2007 (http://www.washingtonpost.com/wp-dyn/content/article/2007/03/06/AR2007030602145.html).

[174] Hirsi Ali, "Obama Should Speak Truth to Islam Because Others Can't," *The Australian*, June 15, 2009 (http://www.aei.org/article/society-and-culture/religion/obama-should-speak-truth-to-islam-because-others-cant/).

[175] Chesler, "Muslims Attack Hindus in India: A Warning for the West? Part I," *PJ Media*, September 13, 2010 (http://pjmedia.com/phyllischesler/2010/09/13/muslims-attack-hindus-in-india-part-i/).

[176] "India's Muslims Expected to Grow at Slower Rate: Report," *Deccan Herald*, January 28, 2011 (http://www.deccanherald.com/content/132619/muslim-population-india-rise-1.html).

[177] Goldberg, "The Rise in Anti-Muslim Hate Crime (and a Startling Omission)," *The Atlantic*, November 22, 2011 (http://www.theatlantic.com/national/archive/2011/11/the-rise-in-anti-muslim-hate-crime-and-a-startling-omission/248494/).

[178] "Obama Moves to De-Link Terrorism from Islam," *New America Media*, April 23, 2010 (http://newamericamedia.org/2010/04/obama-moves-to-de-link-terrorism-from-islam.php).

[179] Lieberman, "Who's the Enemy in the War on Terror," *The Wall Street Journal*, June 15, 2010 (http://lieberman.senate.gov/index.cfm/blog/whos-the-enemy-in-the-war-on-terror).

[180] Lieberman, "Who's the Enemy in the War on Terror," *The Wall Street Journal*, June 15, 2010 (http://lieberman.senate.gov/index.cfm/blog/whos-the-enemy-in-the-war-on-terror).

[181] See, for example, "Country Briefing: Israel-Palestine," *Flashpoints: Guide to World Conflicts* (http://www.flashpoints.info/CB-Israel-Palestine.html).

[182] See Nkwocha, "Myopia Leads to Genocide in Ivory Coast," *Modern Ghana*, April 5, 2011 (http://www.modernghana.com/news/323167/1/myopia-leads-to-genocide-in-ivory-coast.html); Kerby, "Sudan Christians Facing Genocide, Bishop Pleads for Worldwide Prayer," *beliefnet*, June 25, 2011 (http://blog.beliefnet.com/pray_for_the_persecuted_church/2011/06/sudan-christians-facing-genocide-bishop-pleads-for-worldwide-prayer.html); Weinstein, "TheDC Video Vault: A Classic Christopher Hitchens Rhetorical Beatdown," *The Daily Caller*, November 30, 2011 (http://dailycaller.com/2011/11/30/thedc-video-vault-a-classic-christopher-hitchens-rhetorical-beatdown/).

[183] Khazoom, "Jews of the Middle East," *Jewish Virtual Library* (http://www.jewishvirtuallibrary.org/jsource/Judaism/mejews.html). .

[184] Bard, "The Arab Boycott," *Jewish Virtual Library*, updated September 27, 2007 (http://www.jewishvirtuallibrary.org/jsource/History/Arab_boycott.html).

[185] Cohen, "1,000,000 Middle Eastern Jews," *reutrcohen.com*, January 15, 2009 (http://www.reutrcohen.com/2009/01/1000000-middle-eastern-jews.html).

[186] Caldwell, "Helen Thomas Tells Jews to 'Go Home', But What About Blacks and Hispanics?" *Wichita Independent Examiner*, June 7, 2010 (http://www.examiner.com/independent-in-wichita/helen-thomas-tells-jews-go-home-but-what-about-blacks-and-hispanics).

187 Shea, "Teach Your Children Well: Classic Anti-Semitic Literature in Arab Schools," *The Weekly Standard*, August 14, 2006 (http://www.hudson.org/index.cfm?fuseaction=publication_details&id=4569).
188 Bostom, "Lara Logan and Egyptian Muslim Jew-Hatred," *American Thinker*, February 17, 2011 (http://www.americanthinker.com/blog/2011/02/lara_logan_and_egyptian_muslim.html).
189 "Partition—August 1947," *GlobalSecurity.org* (http://www.globalsecurity.org/military/world/war/indo-pak-partition2.htm).
190 Bard, "Myths & Facts Online: The War of 1948," *Jewish Virtual Library* (http://www.jewishvirtuallibrary.org/jsource/myths/mf4.html#11).
191 "The Truth About the Palestinian People," *TargetOfOpportunity.com*, (http://www.targetofopportunity.com/palestinian_truth.htm).
192 Silverman, "Obama's Speech: Defending the 'Indefensible'?" *New Jersey Jewish News*, May 25, 2011 (http://njjewishnews.com/article/op-eds/obamas-speech-defending-the-indefensible).
193 "Jerusalem and the Holy Places—Introduction," Israel Ministry of Foreign Affairs, July 5, 1998 (http://www.mfa.gov.il/MFA/Foreign+Relations/Israels+Foreign+Relations+since+1947/1947-1974/Jerusalem+and+the+Holy+Places+-+Introduction.htm?DisplayMode=print).
194 "The Truth About the Palestinian People," *TargetOfOpportunity.com*, (http://www.targetofopportunity.com/palestinian_truth.htm).
195 Littman, "The Forgotten Refugees," *National Review*, December 6, 2002, as published in *FrontPageMag.com* (http://archive.frontpagemag.com/readArticle.aspx?ARTID=20851).
196 *Country Reports on Terrorism 2009*, Chapter 3: State Sponsors of Terrorism, U.S. Department of State, Office of the Coordinator for Counterterrorism, August 5, 2010 (http://www.state.gov/s/ct/rls/crt/2009/140889.htm).
197 "Ahmadinejad's Holocaust Denial and Anti-Israel Rhetoric," *Réalité EU*, October 1, 2007 (http://www.realite-eu.org/site/apps/nlnet/content3.aspx?c=9dJBLLNkGiF&b=2299861&ct=3284361).
198 Gerson, "What Israel Gained in Gaza," *The Washington Post*, January 30, 2009 (http://www.washingtonpost.com/wp-dyn/content/article/2009/01/29/AR2009012903446.html).
199 Weinstein, "TheDC Video Vault: A Classic Christopher Hitchens Rhetorical Beatdown," *The Daily Caller*, November 30, 2011 (http://dailycaller.com/2011/11/30/thedc-video-vault-a-classic-christopher-hitchens-rhetorical-beatdown/).

www.ingramcontent.com/pod-product-compliance
Lightning Source LLC
Chambersburg PA
CBHW050113280326
41933CB00010B/1077